2 March 2015

THE CHRYSOSTOM BIBLE
A Commentary Series for Preaching and Teaching
Isaiah: A Commentary

p. 20-21

1 - 39   First   The Oracle
40-55   Second   The Destruction
56-66   Third   The Hope

THE CHRYSOSTOM BIBLE
A Commentary Series for Preaching and Teaching

Isaiah: A Commentary

Paul Nadim Tarazi

OCABS PRESS
ST PAUL, MINNESOTA 55124
2013

THE CHRYSOSTOM BIBLE
ISAIAH: A COMMENTARY

ISBN 1-60191-023-1

Other Books by the Author

I Thessalonians: A Commentary

Galatians: A Commentary

The Old Testament: An Introduction

Volume 1: Historical Traditions, revised edition

Volume 2: Prophetic Traditions

Volume 3: Psalms and Wisdom

The New Testament: An Introduction

Volume 1: Paul and Mark

Volume 2: Luke and Acts

Volume 3: Johannine Writings

Volume 4: Matthew and the Canon

The Chrysostom Bible

Genesis: A Commentary

Philippians: A Commentary

Romans: A Commentary

Colossians & Philemon: A Commentary

1 Corinthians: A Commentary

Ezekiel: A Commentary

Joshua: A Commentary

2 Corinthians: A Commentary

Land and Covenant

The Chrysostom Bible
Isaiah: A Commentary

ISBN 1-60191-023-1

Published by OCABS Press, St. Paul, Minnesota.
Printed in the United States of America.

Books are available through OCABS Press at special discounts
for bulk purchases in the United States by academic institutions,
churches, and other organizations. For more information please
email OCABS Press at press@ocabs.org.

Abbreviations

Books by the Author

1 Thess   *1 Thessalonians: A Commentary,* Crestwood, NY: St. Vladimir's Seminary Press, 1982

Gal   *Galatians: A Commentary,* Crestwood, NY: St. Vladimir's Seminary Press, 1994

OTI₁   *The Old Testament: An Introduction, Volume 1: Historical Traditions,* revised edition, Crestwood, NY: St. Vladimir's Seminary Press, 2003

OTI₂   *The Old Testament: An Introduction, Volume 2: Prophetic Traditions,* Crestwood, NY: St. Vladimir's Seminary Press, 1994

OTI₃   *The Old Testament: An Introduction, Volume 3: Psalms and Wisdom,* Crestwood, NY: St. Vladimir's Seminary Press, 1996

NTI₁   *The New Testament: An Introduction, Volume 1: Paul and Mark,* Crestwood, NY: St. Vladimir's Seminary Press, 1999

NTI₂   *The New Testament: An Introduction, Volume 2: Luke and Acts,* Crestwood, NY: St. Vladimir's Seminary Press, 2001

NTI₃   *The New Testament: An Introduction, Volume 3: Johannine Writings,* Crestwood, NY: St. Vladimir's Seminary Press, 2004

NTI₄   *The New Testament: An Introduction, Volume 4: Matthew and the Canon,* St. Paul, MN: OCABS Press, 2009

C-Gen   *Genesis: A Commentary.* The Chrysostom Bible. St. Paul, MN: OCABS Press, 2009

C-Phil   *Philippians: A Commentary.* The Chrysostom Bible. St. Paul, MN: OCABS Press, 2009

C-Rom   *Romans: A Commentary.* The Chrysostom Bible. St. Paul, MN: OCABS Press, 2010

C-Col   *Colossians & Philemon: A Commentary.* The Chrysostom Bible. St. Paul, MN: OCABS Press, 2010

C-1Cor   *1 Corinthians: A Commentary.* The Chrysostom Bible. St. Paul, MN: OCABS Press, 2011

C-Ezek   *Ezekiel: A Commentary.* The Chrysostom Bible. St. Paul, MN: OCABS Press, 2012

C-Josh   *Joshua: A Commentary.* The Chrysostom Bible. St. Paul, MN: OCABS Press, 2013

C-2Cor   *2 Corinthians: A Commentary.* The Chrysostom Bible. St. Paul, MN: OCABS Press, 2013

LAC   *Land and Covenant,* St. Paul, MN: OCABS Press, 2009

Abbreviations

Books of the Old Testament*

Gen	Genesis	Job	Job	Hab	Habakkuk
Ex	Exodus	Ps	Psalms	Zeph	Zephaniah
Lev	Leviticus	Prov	Proverbs	Hag	Haggai
Num	Numbers	Eccl	Ecclesiastes	Zech	Zechariah
Deut	Deuteronomy	Song	Song of Solomon	Mal	Malachi
Josh	Joshua	Is	Isaiah	Tob	Tobit
Judg	Judges	Jer	Jeremiah	Jdt	Judith
Ruth	Ruth	Lam	Lamentations	Wis	Wisdom
1 Sam	1 Samuel	Ezek	Ezekiel	Sir	Sirach (Ecclesiasticus)
2 Sam	2 Samuel	Dan	Daniel	Bar	Baruch
1 Kg	1 Kings	Hos	Hosea	1 Esd	1 Esdras
2 Kg	2 Kings	Joel	Joel	2 Esd	2 Esdras
1 Chr	1 Chronicles	Am	Amos	1 Macc	1 Maccabees
2 Chr	2 Chronicles	Ob	Obadiah	2 Macc	2 Maccabees
Ezra	Ezra	Jon	Jonah	3 Macc	3 Maccabees
Neh	Nehemiah	Mic	Micah	4 Macc	4 Maccabees
Esth	Esther	Nah	Nahum		

Books of the New Testament

Mt	Matthew	Eph	Ephesians	Heb	Hebrews
Mk	Mark	Phil	Philippians	Jas	James
Lk	Luke	Col	Colossians	1 Pet	1 Peter
Jn	John	1 Thess	1 Thessalonians	2 Pet	2 Peter
Acts	Acts	2 Thess	2 Thessalonians	1 Jn	1 John
Rom	Romans	1 Tim	1 Timothy	2 Jn	2 John
1 Cor	1 Corinthians	2 Tim	2 Timothy	3 Jn	3 John
2 Cor	2 Corinthians	Titus	Titus	Jude	Jude
Gal	Galatians	Philem	Philemon	Rev	Revelation

*Following the larger canon known as the Septuagint.

Contents

Preface   15

Introduction   19

1 The Vision of Isaiah   25

Two Superscriptions · A Tripartite Book of Isaiah · Divine Punishment · The Vanity of the Temple Service and Sacrifices · The Harlot Zion and Its Restoration · Jerusalem · Zion

2 Why the Call of the Prophet?   59

The Lord's Vineyard

3 The Call of Isaiah   73

The Sign of še'ar-yašub [A remnant shall return] · The Messianic Sign of Immanuel · The Sign of maher-šalal-ḥaš-baz [The spoil speeds, the prey hastes] · Immanuel · The Second Messianic Sign · Samaria and the Northern Kingdom · The Messianic Prophecy of Universal Peace · Psalm of Praise

4 Oracles concerning the Nations   103

Babylon · The King of Babylon · Egypt · Ashdod · The Sons of Ishmael · Jerusalem · Shebna · Tyre

5 God is King of Judah and all the Nations   125

6 God's Salvation   131

God's Word concerning Samaria · God's Word concerning Jerusalem · The Disobedience of the House of David

7 The Divine Word   143

The Word of God · The Lord is the Universal God · The Redemption of Israel

8 The Servant Poems   153

The First Servant Poem · The Second Servant Poem ·"Israel" in Isaiah · The Third Servant Poem · The Fourth Servant Poem · Sarah, the New Zion · Excursus: The Identity of the Servant of the Poems

9 Post-Exilic Zion   197

Further Reading   209

Preface

The present Bible Commentary Series is not so much in
honor of John Chrysostom as it is to continue and promote
his legacy as an interpreter of the biblical texts for preaching and
teaching God's congregation, in order to prod its members to
proceed on the way they started when they accepted God's
calling. Chrysostom's virtual uniqueness is that he did not
subscribe to any hermeneutic or methodology, since this would
amount to introducing an extra-textual authority over the
biblical texts. For him, scripture is its own interpreter. Listening
to the texts time and again allowed him to realize that "call" and
"read (aloud)" are not interconnected realities; rather, they are
one reality since they both are renditions of the same Hebrew
verb *qara'.* Given that words read aloud are words of instruction
for one "to do them," the only valid reaction would be to hear,
listen, obey, and abide by these words. All these connotations are
subsumed in the same Hebrew verb *šama'.* On the other hand,
these scriptural "words of life" are presented as readily
understandable utterances of a father to his children (Isaiah 1:2-
3). The recipients are never asked to engage in an intellectual
debate with their divine instructor, or even among themselves, to
fathom what he is saying. The Apostle to the Gentiles followed
in the footsteps of the Prophets to Israel by handing down to
them the Gospel, that is, the Law of God's Spirit through his
Christ (Romans 8:2; Galatians 6:2) as fatherly instruction (1
Corinthians 4:15). He in turn wrote readily understandable
letters to be read aloud. It is in these same footsteps that
Chrysostom followed, having learned from both the Prophets
and Paul that the same "words of life" carry also the sentence of
death at the hand of the scriptural God, Judge of all

(Deuteronomy 28; Joshua 8:32-35; Psalm 82; Matthew 3:4-12; Romans 2:12-16; 1 Corinthians 10:1-11; Revelation 20:11-15).

While theological debates and hermeneutical theories come and go after having fed their proponents and their fans with passing human glory, the Golden Mouth's expository homilies, through the centuries, fed and still feed myriads of believers in so many traditions and countries. Virtually banned from dogmatic treatises, he survives in the hearts of "those who have ears to hear." His success is due to his commitment to exegesis rather than to futile hermeneutics. The latter behaves as someone who dictates on a living organism what it is supposed to be, whereas exegesis submits to that organism and endeavors to decipher it through trial and error. There is as much a far cry between the text and the theories about it as there is between a living organism and the theories about it. The biblical texts are the reality of God imparted through their being read aloud in the midst of the congregation, disregarding the value of the sermon that follows. The sermon, much less a theological treatise, is at best an invitation to hear and obey the text. Assessing the shape of an invitation card has no value whatsoever when it comes to the dinner itself; the guests are fed by the dinner, not by the invitation or its phrasing (Luke 14:16-24; Matthew 22:1-14).

This commentary series does not intend to promote Chrysostom's ideas as a public relation manager would do, but rather to follow in the footsteps of his approach as true children and heirs are expected to do. He used all the contemporary tools at his disposal to communicate God's written instruction to his hearers, as a doctor would with his patients, without spending unnecessary energy on peripheral debates requiring the use of professional jargon incomprehensible to the commoner. The writers of this series will try to do the same: muster to the best of their ability all necessary contemporary knowledge to communicate to the general readers the biblical message without burdening them with data unnecessary for that purpose. Whenever it will be deemed necessary or even helpful to do so, and in order to curtail burdensome and lengthy technical asides within the commentaries, specialized monographs related either to specific topics or to the scriptural background—literary, socio-political, or archeological—will be issued as companions to the series.

Paul Nadim Tarazi
Editor

Introduction

Even a speedy overview of scripture will show that the first book of each section is the most important or the one that sets the tone for the rest of the books in that section. Such is obvious in the case of Genesis as the first book of the Law, Joshua as the opener of the Prior Prophets, Psalms the first book among the Writings,[1] Matthew at the head of the Gospels, and Romans at the outset of the Pauline epistles. If this is so, then the same must apply to Isaiah among the Latter Prophets.

However, as I have shown time and again in my Introduction series and my commentaries, the entire scripture is construed as a "story": the story of how God redresses the unhealthy situation brought about by the persistent disobedience of his "children" and how, against all odds, he fulfills his ultimate plan of realizing a world that functions according to his will, similar to the one he created at the beginning (Gen 1) or, in the words of Isaiah, "new heavens and new earth" (66:22) corresponding to the original "heavens and earth" that were "very good" in God's eyes (Gen 1:31). A closer look will reveal that the actual "story" of disobedience covers the Law (Genesis through Deuteronomy) and the Prior Prophets (Joshua through 2 Kings). The Latter Prophets deal in detail with the entire spectrum of the sins of Israel. They also look ahead giving hope to the hearers that God will have the last word and establish his heavenly Zion in whose bosom he will gather the righteous among his children. Among the Latter Prophets the most impressive individual book is

---

[1] Actually in Luke it is entered as the representative of that section of scripture: "Then he said to them, 'These are my words which I spoke to you, while I was still with you, that everything written about me in the law of Moses and the prophets and the psalms must be fulfilled.'" (24:44)

19

undoubtedly Isaiah since its chronological coverage stretches over
the pre-exilic, exilic, and post-exilic periods. It has in its purview
not only Jacob and Abraham (41:8; 51:2), but also Noah (54:9)
and the garden of Eden (51:3), thus encompassing all of
humanity before the choosing of Abraham. Hence the stress in
Isaiah on the inclusion of the nations, even in the matter of
temple service in the new Zion (66:20-21). Isaiah can well be
viewed, without exaggeration, as a mini-scripture. By the same
token it is no wonder that, besides Genesis—the tone-setting
book for the entire scripture in both its Testaments, and
Psalms—the book of psalmody of the new Zion, Isaiah is the
most quoted Old Testament book in the New Testament.[2]

A few words concerning the structure of Isaiah will allow us to
avoid repetitiveness. First of all, the extensive chronological leap
between the end of chapter 39 and the start of chapter 40 is
readily noticeable. The former ends with the demise of King
Hezekiah in early 7th century B.C. The latter refers to the end of
the Babylonian exile at the hand of the Medo-Persian King
Cyrus around 537 B.C. This warrants a division of the book into
two parts: chapters 1-39 and chapters 40-66. Early on the second
part was referred to as the Book of Consolation after its opening
words: "Comfort (*naḥamu*; console), comfort my people, says
your God." (40:1). In more recent times it was dubbed Deutero-
Isaiah[3] or Second-Isaiah. Then, due to the fact that the content
of chapters 40-55 revolve around the end of the exile proper,
while chapters 56-66 deal with post-exilic Jerusalem and Judah,
scholars opted for referring to the first (chs.40-55) as Deutero-
Isaiah or Second-Isaiah and to the second (chs.56-66) as Trito-

---

[2] It is interesting, in this regard, to further note that those three books are the opening
ones of the Law, the Latter Prophets, and the Writings.
[3] From the Greek *devteros* (second).

Isaiah[4] or Third-Isaiah[5] in order to facilitate reference to each part. I shall abide by this terminology for practical reasons. Whenever I have in mind both sections (chs.40-66) I shall use the phrase "the second part of Isaiah" or "the second part of the book." My readers should bear in mind that this technical division does not take away from the fact that the entirety of Isaiah remains one book as will be made clear in my discussion of the introductory chapter one.

[handwritten annotations:]

1-39   1st Isaiah

40-66 (Book of Comfort)

40-55 Deutero-Isaiah   2nd Isaiah

56-66 Trito-Isaiah   3rd Isaiah

---

[4] From the Greek *tritos* (third).
[5] In the commentary I shall show that each of these two sections is actually a separate literary unit.

Part I

Isaiah Chapters 1-39

Chapter 1
The Vision of Isaiah

Two Superscriptions

The vision (*ḥazon*) of Isaiah the son of Amoz, which he saw
(*ḥazah*) concerning ('*al*; against) Judah and Jerusalem in the days
of Uzziah, Jotham, Ahaz, and Hezekiah, kings of Judah. (1:1)

The word (*dabar*) which Isaiah the son of Amoz saw (*ḥazah*)
concerning ('*al*; against) Judah and Jerusalem. (2:1)

A common feature of prophetic books is the superscription,
which is an initial sentence or two that introduces the
prophet, often with a brief genealogy, includes the period of the
prophet's activity, and identifies his message as a word or vision
from God. In essence, the superscription acts as the title of the
book. A striking feature of Isaiah is its double superscription or
double title, just one chapter apart. Two questions come
simultaneously to mind: "Why two titles or two introductions?"
and "Why the discrepancy as to what Isaiah saw?" A glance at the
book will show the following:

1. the verb *ḥazah* in the third person singular is
    used exclusively with Isaiah as subject (1:1; 2:1;
    13:1)

2. although the object of *ḥazah* is a vision in 1:1, in
    the following two instances it is a "word" (*dabar*;
    2:1) or an oracle (*maśśah*; 13:1)

3. the noun *ḥazon* without any further qualification
    occurs only in 1:1.[1]

The immediate conclusion is that Isaiah alone is privy to a
"vision" in which an aural message is communicated. In other
words, it is not a "vision" that is bound to the recipient's
interpretation.[2] The basic connotation of "seeing" when a
message is communicated is that of closeness and intimacy and,
at the extreme, of privacy. This connotation is still applicable in
modern languages. For example, one says, "The bishop gave me
an audience, so I was able to see him." Such sight would not be
more valuable than speaking with him over the telephone if the
audience did not entail any conversation! The value of "seeing"
the bishop lies in that one was not only able to be "in his
presence" and but also to *converse* with him "face to face" or,
more à propos, listen to him at close range. This is precisely what
occurs in Isaiah, and is confirmed by the fact that the summons
in Isaiah's "vision" has an *aural* content: "Hear, O heavens, and
give ear, O earth; for the Lord has spoken" (1:2b).[3] It is further
spelled out in the second title or superscription where Isaiah is
said to have "seen" a "word" (2:1).

---

[1] The other instance of that noun has a negative connotation: "And the multitude of
all the nations that fight against Ariel, all that fight against her and her stronghold and
distress her, shall be like a dream, a vision (*ḥazon*) of the night." (Is 29:7)

[2] Such personal interpretation developed in mystical theology under the influence of
Platonism and, more so, Plotinism.

[3] Isaiah is not a unique case; compare with Ezek 1:1-3: "In the thirtieth year, in the
fourth month, on the fifth day of the month, as I was among the exiles by the river
Chebar, the heavens were opened, and *I saw visions of God*. On the fifth day of the
month (it was the fifth year of the exile of King Jehoiachin), *the word of the Lord came
to Ezekiel* the priest, the son of Buzi, in the land of the Chaldeans by the river Chebar;
and the hand of the Lord was upon him there."

The intention behind the use of "vision" in 1:1 is to differentiate God's chosen emissary from the pseudo-prophets who are said to have either false or fabricated visions of their own. This is precisely what we find in Jeremiah and Ezekiel:

> And the Lord said to me: "The prophets are prophesying lies in my name; I did not send them, nor did I command them or speak to them. They are prophesying to you a lying vision (*ḥazon*), worthless divination, and the deceit of their own minds." (Jer 14:14)

> Therefore thus says the Lord of hosts concerning the prophets: "Behold, I will feed them with wormwood, and give them poisoned water to drink; for from the prophets of Jerusalem ungodliness has gone forth into all the land." Thus says the Lord of hosts: "Do not listen to the words of the prophets who prophesy to you, filling you with vain hopes; they speak visions (*ḥazon*; vision) of their own minds, not from the mouth of the Lord." (Jer 23:15-16)

> Thus will I spend my wrath upon the wall, and upon those who have daubed it with whitewash; and I will say to you, The wall is no more, nor those who daubed it, the prophets of Israel who prophesied concerning Jerusalem and saw (*ḥozim*) visions (*ḥazon*; vision) of peace for her, when there was no peace, says the Lord God. (Ezek 13:15-16)

> Son of man, what is this proverb that you have about the land of Israel, saying, "The days grow long, and every vision (*ḥazon*) comes to nought"? Tell them therefore, "Thus says the Lord God: I will put an end to this proverb, and they shall no more use it as a proverb in Israel." But say to them, The days are at hand, and the fulfilment of every vision (*ḥazon*). For there shall be no more any false vision (*ḥazon*) or flattering divination within the house of Israel. (Ezek 12:22-24)

In Isaiah the sinful Jerusalem that opposed the prophet is addressed pejoratively as "the valley of vision (*ḥizzayon*)" (22:1, 5).[4] By using another noun, although from the same root as *ḥazon*, the author is drawing the hearer's attention to the fact that the false prophets of Jerusalem are not privy to the same "vision" as Isaiah (1:1; 2:1).

The split into two superscriptions is intended to announce as well as bring together the message of the book that is clearly divided into two parts, each dealing with a period of time far removed from the other. Hezekiah, the last of the four kings referred to in 1:1, whose reign straddles the end of the eighth century and the beginning of the seventh century B.C., is heard of again in the last verse of chapter 39 which ends the first part of the book: "Then said Hezekiah to Isaiah, 'The word of the Lord which you have spoken is good.' For he thought, 'There will be peace and security in my days.'" (v.8) The second part of the book opens with the announcement of the end of the Babylonian exile (40:1-2) brought about by the Medo-Persian King Cyrus who is mentioned by name as the fulfiller of God's purpose to rebuild Jerusalem (Is 44:28-45:1; see also 2 Chr 36:22-23; Ezra 1:1-2) that was punished "double for her sins" (Is 40:2). That event took place one and a half centuries after Hezekiah's death. Given that the second part of the book is under the overarching umbrella of 1:1, it appears that Isaiah is saying things about events that will take place at a much later time, even after his demise. In view of this, it stands to reason that the author would opt for the term "vision" in the title for the entire book, particularly since the last chapter of the book speaks of end times when priests and Levites will be taken from

---

[4] These are the only instances of that noun in Isaiah.

among the nations in the redeemed Jerusalem (66:18-21). Still, in order to make sure that the hearers would not imagine that Isaiah's vision is a projection of his own mind, after the introductory chapter to the entire book the author prefaces Isaiah's actual activity with another introduction making it clear that the prophet received a "word" (2:1) that eventually will be consigned to a scroll (8:16), just as with Ezekiel (1:1-3; 2:1-3:11). The choice of "word" is very appropriate given that Second-Isaiah (chs.40-55) revolves, as we shall see, around "the divine word" (40:8; 55:11).

A Tripartite Book of Isaiah

As an introduction to the entire book, chapter 1 reflects the book's structure. After a critique of the sins of the people (1:2-23), which corresponds to the first part of the book (chs.2-39), we hear of a corrective punishment (1:24-25) whose outcome is the redeemed Jerusalem (vv.26-27), which reflects the content of the second book (chs.40-66). However, since the redemption will be founded on justice (*mišpaṭ*; just judgment) and righteousness (*ṣedaqah*; legal righteousness; innocence before the law; 1:27), the chapter ends on a note of threat against the potential ill-doers (vv.28-31), a note that is reminiscent of the critique of vv.2-23. Looking more closely at chapters 40-66 one will notice that they are divided into two subsections: in chapters 40-55 redemption revolves around the divine word and thus is exclusively the work of God; in chapters 56-66 the redeemed city is still prey to unrighteousness and wickedness (56:10-57:13; 58:1-12; 59:1-20; 65:1-66:17), reminiscent of the situation in pre-exilic Samaria and Jerusalem (chs.2-39). That is why ultimate salvation (66:18-23) will nevertheless include judgment

followed by a purge (v.24).[5] Thus the introductory chapter is
constructed in a way that "predicts" the structure of the book
itself, a fitting expectation of an introduction. Such "prediction"
finds corroboration in that 1:27 (Zion shall be redeemed by
justice, and those in her who repent, by *righteousness*) is echoed in
the opening verse of chapters 56-66 (Thus says the Lord: "Keep
justice (*mišpaṭ*), and do righteousness (*ṣedaqah*), for soon my
salvation[6] will come, and my deliverance[7] be revealed"). In
addition, the negative connotation of "gardens" finds its echo in
two instances found at the end of Isaiah:

For you shall be ashamed of the oaks in which you delighted; and
you shall blush for the gardens which you have chosen. (1:29)

I spread out my hands all the day to a rebellious people, who walk
in a way that is not good, following their own devices; a people
who provoke me to my face continually, sacrificing in gardens and
burning incense upon bricks. (65:2-3)

For behold, the Lord will come in fire, and his chariots like the
stormwind, to render his anger in fury, and his rebuke with flames
of fire. For by fire will the Lord execute judgment, and by his
sword, upon all flesh; and those slain by the Lord shall be many.
Those who sanctify and purify themselves to go into the gardens,

---

[5] Such is not a unique instance. The classic text is found in Ezekiel: "I will bring you
out from the peoples and gather you out of the countries where you are scattered, with
a mighty hand and an outstretched arm, and with wrath poured out; and I will bring
you into the wilderness of the peoples, and there I will enter into judgment with you
face to face. As I entered into judgment with your fathers in the wilderness of the land
of Egypt, so I will enter into judgment with you, says the Lord God. I will make you
pass under the rod, and I will let you go in by number. I will purge out the rebels from
among you, and those who transgress against me; I will bring them out of the land
where they sojourn, but they shall not enter the land of Israel. Then you will know
that I am the Lord." (20:34-38)

[6] Salvation corresponds to the redemption of 1:27.

[7] The Hebrew original is *ṣedaqah*. I shall discuss this matter later.

following one in the midst, eating swine's flesh and the abomination and mice, shall come to an end together, says the Lord. (66:15-17)[8]

Is there an indication, as in the case of chapters 40-55, that chapters 55-66 constitute a sub-section? I believe there is. Just as "the divine word" brackets the former, the concern with the inclusion of the "foreigners" in the new Jerusalem brackets the latter:

Comfort, comfort my people, says your God. Speak tenderly to Jerusalem, and cry to her that her warfare is ended that her iniquity is pardoned, that she has received from the Lord's hand double for all her sins. A voice cries: In the wilderness prepare the way of the Lord, make straight in the desert a highway for our God. Every valley shall be lifted up and every mountain and hill be made low; the uneven ground shall become level, and the rough places a plain. And the glory of the Lord shall be revealed, and all flesh shall see it together, for the mouth of the Lord has spoken. A voice says, "Cry!" and I said, "What shall I cry?" All flesh is grass, and all its beauty is like the flower of the field. The grass withers, the flower fades, when the breath of the Lord blows upon it; surely the people is grass. The grass withers, the flower fades; but the word of our God will stand for ever. (40:1-8)

Incline your ear, and come to me; hear, that your soul may live; and I will make with you an everlasting covenant ... For my thoughts are not your thoughts, neither are your ways my ways, says the Lord. For as the heavens are higher than the earth, so are my ways higher than your ways and my thoughts than your thoughts. For as the rain and the snow come down from heaven, and return not thither but water the earth, making it bring forth

---

[8] Notice how this passage includes a reference to judgment by fire, which is also found at the end of Is 1: "And the strong shall become tow, and his work a spark, and both of them shall burn together, with none to quench them." (v.31)

and sprout, giving seed to the sower and bread to the eater, so shall my word be that goes forth from my mouth; it shall not return to me empty, but it shall accomplish that which I purpose, and prosper in the thing for which I send it. (55:3, 8-11)

Let not the foreigner who has joined himself to the Lord say, "The Lord will surely separate me from his people"; and let not the eunuch say, "Behold, I am a dry tree." For thus says the Lord: "To the eunuchs who keep my sabbaths, who choose the things that please me and hold fast my covenant, I will give in my house and within my walls a monument and a name better than sons and daughters; I will give them an everlasting name which shall not be cut off. "And the foreigners who join themselves to the Lord, to minister to him, to love the name of the Lord, and to be his servants, every one who keeps the sabbath, and does not profane it, and holds fast my covenant—these I will bring to my holy mountain, and make them joyful in my house of prayer; their burnt offerings and their sacrifices will be accepted on my altar; for my house shall be called a house of prayer for all peoples. (56:3-7)

I am coming to gather all nations and tongues; and they shall come and shall see my glory, and I will set a sign among them. And from them I will send survivors to the nations, to Tarshish, Put, and Lud, who draw the bow, to Tubal and Javan, to the coastlands afar off, that have not heard my fame or seen my glory; and they shall declare my glory among the nations. And they shall bring all your brethren from all the nations as an offering to the Lord, upon horses, and in chariots, and in litters, and upon mules, and upon dromedaries, to my holy mountain Jerusalem, says the Lord, just as the Israelites bring their cereal offering in a clean vessel to the house of the Lord. And some of them also I will take for priests and for Levites, says the Lord. (66:18b-21)

So the movement of the Isaianic story covers three acts: (1) Israel's disobedience that leads to (2) its punishment in the form of its people being scattered among the nations, which in turn results in (3) the gathering of the nations together with the redeemed of Israel.[9] That the third act is foreseen in the second can be heard in chapters 40-55:

> Behold my servant, whom I uphold, my chosen, in whom my soul delights; I have put my Spirit upon him, he will bring forth justice to the nations ... He will not fail or be discouraged till he has established justice in the earth; and the coastlands wait for his law. Thus says God, the Lord, who created the heavens and stretched them out, who spread forth the earth and what comes from it, who gives breath to the people upon it and spirit to those who walk in it: "I am the Lord, I have called you in righteousness, I have taken you by the hand and kept you; I have given you as a covenant to the people, a light to the nations, to open the eyes that are blind, to bring out the prisoners from the dungeon, from the prison those who sit in darkness." (42:1, 4-7)

> Listen to me, O coastlands, and hearken, you peoples from afar. The Lord called me from the womb, from the body of my mother he named my name. He made my mouth like a sharp sword, in the shadow of his hand he hid me; he made me a polished arrow, in his quiver he hid me away. And he said to me, "You are my servant, Israel, in whom I will be glorified." ... he says: "It is too light a thing that you should be my servant to raise up the tribes of Jacob and to restore the preserved of Israel; I will give you as a light to the nations, that my salvation may reach to the end of the earth." (49:1-3, 6)

---

[9] This divine "plan" is behind Paul's teaching in Romans 9-11.

The Sin of Jerusalem and Its Leaders

The indictment against Jerusalem is divided into four parts: (1) repeated disobedience (1:2-4); (2) divine punishment (vv.3-9); (3) vain temple service (vv.11-20); (4) injustice on the part of its leaders (vv.21-23).

Since the Lord is taking the role of an accuser (v.2), the prophet issues a call for two witnesses, as required by the Law in the case of an execution (Deut 17:6; 19:15). The two witnesses are chosen as a "pair." In languages "pairs," whether complementary, such as "heavens and earth," "men and women," "adults and children," "humans and animals," "fauna and flora," or opposite, such as "black and white," "light and darkness," "day and night," "rich and poor," "big and small," are intended to speak of a totality rather than two independent parts. Thus each "pair" is not to be understood as a combination of two individual entities, rather it is reflective of the idea of "everything." In the case of the pair "heavens and earth" the totality is that of the entire human realm, functionally speaking. Man lives on earth; the heavens are the source of rain essential for his daily life as well as the locale of his deities and of the sun and moon that control the cycles of the year. By using the literary or poetic split[10] between the two elements in Isaiah 1:2, the author is making "everything there is" a valid legal witness to God's accusation against his people. The prophet as a herald is calling upon the witnesses to also act as judge and jury between the Lord and his children.

---

[10] Such a literary or poetic split can be seen in Ps 8:3 (When I look at thy heavens, the work of thy fingers, the moon and the stars which thou hast established); 19:1 (The heavens are telling the glory of God; and the firmament proclaims his handiwork); 33:6 (By the word of the Lord the heavens were made, and all their host by the breath of his mouth); 36:5 (Thy steadfast love, O Lord, extends to the heavens, thy faithfulness to the clouds).

[2]Hear, O heavens, and give ear, O earth; for the Lord has spoken; "Sons have I reared and brought up, but they have rebelled against me. [3]The ox knows its owner, and the ass its master's crib; but Israel does not know, my people does not understand." [4]Ah, sinful nation, a people laden with iniquity, offspring of evildoers, sons who deal corruptly! They have forsaken the Lord, they have despised the Holy One of Israel, they are utterly estranged. [5]Why will you still be smitten that you continue to rebel? The whole head is sick, and the whole heart faint. [6]From the sole of the foot even to the head, there is no soundness in it, but bruises and sores and bleeding wounds; they are not pressed out, or bound up, or softened with oil. [7]Your country lies desolate, your cities are burned with fire; in your very presence aliens devour your land; it is desolate, as overthrown by aliens. [8]And the daughter of Zion is left like a booth in a vineyard, like a lodge in a cucumber field, like a besieged city. [9]If the Lord of hosts had not left us a few survivors, we should have been like Sodom, and become like Gomorrah.

As expounded in most of the prophets,[11] Israel's sin is essentially that of *peša'* (Is 1:2), which is the rebellion of children against the authority of their father, an action that disturbs the order and the "peace" (*šalom*) necessary for the maintenance of life within the family, clan or tribe. This explains why the obliteration of such wickedness is necessary for the final divine restoration of peace (11:1-9).

Isaiah 1:3 is magisterially fashioned to ensure that the hearer unconditionally support the Lord's cause. It brings into the picture another "pair," a metaphor for the totality of the animal realm, underscoring the message that even animals are more respectful toward their owners who feed and care for them than God's own children are toward him. Listening again more

---

[11] See, e.g., Is 1:28; Jer 2:8, 29; Ezek 2:3; Hos 7:13; 8:1; Am 1:3, 6, 9, 11, 13; Mic 1:5 [twice], 13; Zeph 3:11.

carefully to the original, one will notice that the verse is richer
than it sounds at first hearing:

1. The choice of animals looks ahead to the era of
    peace under the tutelage of God's chosen one
    (11:1-9). Though the animal realm will be under
    control (vv.6-8), the human realm will have to be
    purged: "... with righteousness he shall judge the
    poor, and decide with equity for the meek of the
    earth; and he shall smite the earth with the rod of
    his mouth, and with the breath of his lips he shall
    slay the wicked." (v.4) Then "the earth shall be
    full of the knowledge (*de'ah*) of the Lord" (v.9),
    which knowledge was lacking among humans
    though already extant among animals: "The ox
    knows (*yada'*) its owner, and the ass its master's
    crib; but Israel does not know (*yada'*), my people
    does not understand." (1:3)

2. Moreover "owner" (*qoneh*) and "master" (*ba'al*)
    (1:3) also look ahead to their later use in
    conjunction with God's act of restoration.
    Owner (*qoneh*) is used in the messianic text of
    chapter 11: "In that day the root of Jesse shall
    stand as an ensign to the peoples; him shall the
    nations seek, and his dwellings shall be glorious.
    In that day the Lord will extend his hand yet a
    second time to recover (*qenot*)[12] the remnant
    which is left of his people, from Assyria, from
    Egypt, from Pathros, from Ethiopia, from Elam,

---

[12] The intentionality of the connection is evident in that 11:11 is the only instance of
the root *qanah* in reference to God in Isaiah.

from Shinar, from Hamath, and from the coastlands of the sea." (vv.10-11) The Lord will behave as the owner of "the remnant of his people" after having purged the wicked (v.4b); he will reinstate his lordship over the recalcitrant people (1:3b) and make them obedient like the ox (1:3a; 11:7b).[13] Similarly the root *ba'al* is found later as God reestablishes his upper hand over Israel: "For your Maker is your husband (*ba'al*), the Lord of hosts is his name; and the Holy One of Israel is your Redeemer, the God of the whole earth he is called." (54:5)[14]

The people's recurrent disobedience is reflected in a series of four phrases clustered in two pairs, the first: "Ah, sinful (*hote'*) nation, a people laden with iniquity (*'awon*)" (1:4a), and the second: "offspring of evildoers (*mere'im*), sons who deal corruptly (*mashitim*)!" (1:4b) *hote'* is from the same root as *hatta't* whose technical meaning is "trespass" (infraction) and is the most common term for "sin" in scripture. *'awon* (burden) has the same connotation as the English word "guilt" and is often

---

[13] In 1:3a we have the Hebrew *šor* which is specifically "ox," whereas 11:7b has the Hebrew *baqar* meaning cattle. Actually the entire verse 7 reads: "The cow (*parah*) and the bear shall feed; their young shall lie down together; and the lion shall eat straw like the ox (*baqar*, cattle)."

[14] On the one hand, a god, as father of the citizens, was considered as the husband of his city; the city, in turn, would be the mother of the citizens. On the other hand, in a patriarchal society, the husband would be the "master" of the household which includes his wife, and thus he would "rule over her" (Gen 3:16). At his death, if the children were still minor, his widow would become the "mistress" (*ba'alah*) of the house[hold], just as was the case in the Roman empire: "So he arose and went to Zarephath; and when he came to the gate of the city, behold, a widow was there gathering sticks ... After this the son of the woman, *the mistress of the house* (*ba'alat habbayt*), became ill; and his illness was so severe that there was no breath left in him." (1 Kg 17:10a, 17)

translated as such; it reflects both the sinful action and the responsibility therefor and thus the punishment it entails. Depending on the context, RSV renders it as either "guilt" or "punishment." In scripture the pairing of those two common terms, i.e., *ḥoṭe'* and *'awon*, reflects consummate iniquity. However coupling the first pair with another pair makes the total number of terms four, an indication of universality. So the hearer of the original cannot miss the author's expressed intention to underscore that the *peša'* (rebellion) of Israel is so widespread that it has reached an unsurpassed peak. This is tantamount to "forsaking the Lord" and "despising the Holy One of Israel" (v.4cd). While the phrase "forsaking the Lord" is classic in scripture, "the Holy One of Israel" is special to Isaiah; it occurs twenty five times in this book compared to a total of six times in the rest of scripture. This is understandable since the God who called the prophet is described as the thrice holy Lord (6:3).

Finally, what we discovered earlier concerning 1:3a, that is, looking ahead to the reversal of the state of rebellion in the age of peace (11:1-9), finds corroboration in that the behavior of evildoing (*mere'im*) and dealing corruptly (*mašḥitim*) of 1:4b will be redressed then: "They shall not hurt (*yare'u*; behave in an evil way) or destroy (*yašḥitu*) in all my holy mountain." (11:9a) The same thought is also found at the end of the book when the nations will join the remnant of Israel as children of the new Jerusalem: "The wolf and the lamb shall feed together, the lion shall eat straw like the ox; and dust shall be the serpent's food. They shall not hurt (*yare'u*) or destroy (*yašḥitu*) in all my holy mountain, says the Lord." (65:25) This, in turn, confirms that the movement of the Isaianic story covers three acts: Israel's disobedience, then its punishment in the form of the people

being scattered among the nations, and finally the gathering of
the nations together with the redeemed of Israel. The Book of
Isaiah is a tightly knit work of literature. It opens with the
disturbance of God's universal peace (2:2-5) brought about by
the disobedience of Jacob, and it ends with God reestablishing
that peace in spite of Jacob's sin. In this sense, Isaiah is a "mini-
scripture."

Divine Punishment

A city's siege is usually an omen for its total destruction and
the annihilation of its inhabitants. This is done through four
elements: sickness (pestilence), famine, sword (death), or
eventual (death in) exile (Ezek 5:12). Since Isaiah is addressing
Jerusalem and, by extension, Judah, the most fitting metaphor of
divine punishment for disobedience is the siege, as is expressed in
the Law (Deut 28:47-68) and clearly reflected in Isaiah 1:7-8.
However, in order to bring the message home to each and every
person, the prophet expands on sickness, the first of the four
elements: "Why will you still be smitten, that you continue to
rebel? The whole head is sick, and the whole heart faint. From
the sole of the foot even to the head, there is no soundness in it,
but bruises and sores and bleeding wounds; they are not pressed
out, or bound up, or softened with oil." (Is 1:5-6) Still, the real
harshness in the picture is that Jerusalem is compared to Sodom
and Gomorrah (v.9b), which brings to mind a total and full end.
If a few survivors are left, such is neither happenstance nor a
miscalculation by the Assyrians who besieged Jerusalem (7:17-
25; 36:1-37:20); it is the work of "the Lord of hosts" (1:9a) and,
if so, then it is that same Lord who conducted the siege. This is
precisely what we hear in the indictment from the Lord of hosts
himself wherein the leaders of Jerusalem are identified as his
personal enemies and foes and that he will wage war against

them: "Therefore the Lord says, the Lord of hosts, the Mighty One (*'abbir*) of Israel: 'Ah, I will vent my wrath on my enemies, and avenge myself on my foes. I will turn my hand against you and will smelt away your dross as with lye and remove all your alloy.'" (vv.24-25)[15] And it is the same God, "the Mighty One (*'abbir*) of Jacob," who will prove to be the protector of the redeemed Jerusalem: "I will make your oppressors eat their own flesh, and they shall be drunk with their own blood as with wine. Then all flesh shall know that I am the Lord your Savior, and your Redeemer, the Mighty One (*'abbir*) of Jacob" (49:26); "You shall suck the milk of nations, you shall suck the breast of kings; and you shall know that I, the Lord, am your Savior and your Redeemer, the Mighty One (*'abbir*) of Jacob." (60:16)

The Vanity of the Temple Service and Sacrifices

[10]Hear the word of the Lord, you rulers of Sodom! Give ear to the teaching of our God, you people of Gomorrah! [11]What to me is the multitude of your sacrifices? says the Lord; I have had enough of your burnt offerings of rams and the fat of fed beasts; I do not delight in the blood of bulls, or of lambs, or of he-goats. [12]When you come to appear before me, who requires of you this trampling of my courts? [13]Bring no more vain offerings; incense is an abomination to me. New moon and sabbath and the calling of assemblies—I cannot endure iniquity and solemn assembly. [14]Your

---

[15] See also the following classic passages, one of which occurs in Isaiah, where God himself is said to be the "enemy" of his own people: "For he said, Surely they are my people, sons who will not deal falsely; and he became their Savior ... But they rebelled and grieved his holy Spirit; therefore he turned to be their enemy, and himself fought against them" (Is 63:8, 10); "'Behold, I will press you down in your place, as a cart full of sheaves presses down. Flight shall perish from the swift, and the strong shall not retain his strength, nor shall the mighty save his life; he who handles the bow shall not stand, and he who is swift of foot shall not save himself, nor shall he who rides the horse save his life; and he who is stout of heart among the mighty shall flee away naked in that day,' says the Lord." (Am 2:13-16)

new moons and your appointed feasts, my soul hates; they have become a burden to me, I am weary of bearing them. [15]When you spread forth your hands, I will hide my eyes from you; even though you make many prayers, I will not listen; your hands are full of blood. [16]Wash yourselves; make yourselves clean; remove the evil of your doings from before my eyes, cease to do evil, [17]learn to do good; seek justice, correct oppression; defend the fatherless, plead for the widow. [18]Come now, let us reason together, says the Lord: though your sins are like scarlet, they shall be as white as snow; though they are red like crimson, they shall be like wool. [19]If you are willing and obedient, you shall eat the good of the land; [20]but if you refuse and rebel, you shall be devoured by the sword; for the mouth of the Lord has spoken.

Sparing Jerusalem from the Assyrian siege (1:9; see 37:21-38) is not only a lesson, but also a warning that the city would be spared in the future only if it is "willing and obedient" (1:19-20). That is why the passage of vv.10-20 starts by addressing Jerusalem as Sodom and Gomorrah (v.10), just as in v.9. Still, beyond the punishment (vv.5-9), v.10 harks back to the beginning of the prophetic message where heavens and earth are called upon as witnesses to the sin of the people: "Hear (*šim'u*), O heavens, and give ear (*ha'azini*), O earth." (v.2a) This time around, the same verbs are used to call upon the leaders of Jerusalem to hear the word of the Lord and give ear to his teaching (law): "Hear (*šim'u*) the word (*dabar*) of the Lord, you rulers of Sodom! Give ear to (*ha'azinu*) the teaching (*torah*; law) of our God, you people of Gomorrah!" (v.10) They and their city will be spared only if they hearken to that word of teaching as is evident from the end statement after the offer to change their practices (vv.19-20a): "for the mouth of the Lord has spoken (*dibber*; from the same root as *dabar*)." (v.20b) Unfortunately, the divine appeal will go unheeded (vv.21-23), and the city will fall at God's hand (vv.24-25). The same hand that *delivered* it *from* the Assyrians will *deliver* it *to* the Babylonians (39:5-7).

The reason behind the harsh invective against temple service and sacrifices (1:11-15a) is that "your hands are full of blood" (v.15b). The meaning of this statement is made clear in the following verses (vv.16-17). Equating disregard for the orphan and the widow with shedding of blood is understandable. Of all people in the Ancient Near East societies, the widow and the orphan were the most in need. In the absence of any social security, they were ultimately the responsibility of the monarch, who was a parent to all citizens in his realm (Ps 72:2, 4, 12-14). Notice how a few verses later the main expression of rebellion is neglecting the widow and the needy (Is 1:23). That is why the Lord of hosts, the true King (6:5), will not be appeased by either the people's or their leaders' (1:10) "lip service" (29:13; see also Jer 7:2-10). What is important to remember is that this ruling concerning vain offerings will still be operative in the temple of the new Jerusalem (66:1-5).

The Harlot Zion and Its Restoration

In scripture the classical metaphor for rebellion against God is harlotry, that is, following other extraneous authorities be they foreign deities, foreign monarchs, or one's own preferences (Ezek 16; 20; Hos 1-2). Being a harlot (*zonah*) is the opposite of being *ne'emanah* (trustworthy; [found] faithful). Unfortunately, the original meaning of scriptural "faith" was adulterated by classical philosophical theology and ended up reflecting a mental attitude—its meaning became tantamount to "belief," that is, an intellectual stand taken by the person who "believes," as well as the outcome (content) of such belief. This is, at best, a far cry from scriptural "trustworthiness." The Semitic root *'aman* connotes a response to a proposition offered by someone else, that is, an endorsement of an offer that aims at the recipient's ultimate safety and well-being, the result of which is also rendered with the same root *'aman*. Since the proposition comes aurally through an uttered "word," the required response is also expressed through the uttered word *'amen* to declare one's trust in the proposition. The archetypical passage is found in Deuteronomy:

> And the Levites shall declare to all the men of Israel with a loud voice: "Cursed be the man who makes a graven or molten image, an abomination to the Lord, a thing made by the hands of a craftsman, and sets it up in secret." And all the people shall answer and say, "Amen." "Cursed be he who dishonors his father or his mother." And all the people shall say, "Amen." "Cursed be he who removes his neighbor's landmark." And all the people shall say, "Amen." "Cursed be he who misleads a blind man on the road." And all the people shall say, "Amen." "Cursed be he who perverts the justice due to the sojourner, the fatherless, and the widow." And all the people shall say, "Amen." "Cursed be he who lies with his father's wife, because he has uncovered her who is his father's." And all the people shall say, "Amen." "Cursed be he who lies with any kind of beast." And all the people shall say, "Amen." "Cursed be he who lies with his sister, whether the daughter of his father or the daughter of his mother." And all the people shall say, "Amen." "Cursed be he who lies with his mother-in-law." And all the people shall say, "Amen." "Cursed be he who slays his neighbor in secret." And all the people shall say, "Amen." "Cursed be he who takes a bribe to slay an innocent person." And all the people shall say, "Amen." "Cursed be he who does not confirm the words of this law by doing them." And all the people shall say, "Amen."(27:14-26)

Endorsing the statement concerning the curse is not enough; indeed, "cursed be he who does not confirm the words of this law *by doing them*" (v.26). So saying "Amen" is not the end of the matter, rather it is just the beginning. In scriptural Greek terminology, saying "Amen" makes someone *pistevōn* (believer, trusting) in what is proposed, but not yet *pistos* ([trust]worthy of the expressed trust). As Paul writes, the one who accepts a commission that is *entrusted* to him is to be *found* "(trust)worthy" (*pistos*) and not *feel*, let alone declare oneself, such:

> For if I do this of my own will, I have a reward; but if not of my own will, I am entrusted (*pepistevmai*) with a commission (*oikonomian*) ... This is how one should regard us, as servants of Christ and stewards (*oikonomous*) of the mysteries of God. Moreover it is required of stewards that they be found (*hevrethē*) trustworthy (*pistos*). But with me it is a very small thing that I should be judged by you or by any human court. I do not even judge myself. I am not aware of anything against myself, but I am not thereby acquitted. It is the Lord who judges me. Therefore do not pronounce judgment before the time, before the Lord comes, who will bring to light the things now hidden in darkness and will disclose the purposes of the heart. Then every man will receive his commendation from God. (1 Cor 9:17; 4:1-5)

This is precisely what we hear in Isaiah. It is the word of the Lord that is declaring the city that was supposed to be *ne'emanah* (trustworthy, faithful) a harlot because his justice (*mišpaṭ*) and righteousness (*ṣedeq*), which were supposed to be adorning her, are nowhere to be *found* (1:21). It is only when she is purged by him (vv.24-25), and he redeems her by justice and righteousness (v.27) that she will become the "city of righteousness," that is to say, the "city where righteousness lodges" (v.21b), and will be granted anew her title of "faithful city" (v.26). My readers are reminded that both *mišpaṭ* (just judgment) and *ṣedeq* (righteousness) are terms pertaining to the Law. This legal aspect is evident in that not all will fare well in the reinstated city since the purge will continue to take its course: "But rebels (*poše'im*; from the same root as *paše'u* [rebelled, v.2]) and sinners (*ḥaṭṭa'im*; compare with "sinful" [*ḥoṭe'*] nation, v.4a) shall be destroyed together, and those who forsake the Lord (compare with v.4b) shall be consumed." (v.28: see in continuation vv.29-31, and also 11:4b and 66:24) This, in turn, explains why in dealing with the new Jerusalem at the end of the book, one encounters the same phraseology of chapter 1:

> But you, draw near hither, sons of the sorceress, offspring of the adulterer and the harlot (*tizneh*: who commits harlotry). Of whom are you making sport? Against whom do you open your mouth wide and put out your tongue? Are you not children of transgression (*peša'*; rebellion), the offspring of deceit, you who burn with lust among the oaks ('*elim*),[16] under every green tree; who slay your children in the valleys, under the clefts of the rocks? (57:3-5)

Jerusalem

Although the book title speaks of Jerusalem, that city is referred to twice as Zion in chapter 1 (vv.8, 27). Is there a functional difference between the two names? Let me start with some statistics. Neither name occurs in the Law. Outside the Pentateuch, Jerusalem is found throughout the rest of the Old Testament. Zion, on the other hand, is virtually confined to the Latter Prophets,[17] the Book of Psalms, and Lamentations.[18]

---

[16] Compare with 1:29a (For you shall be ashamed of the oaks ('*elim*) in which you delighted).

[17] Isaiah, Jeremiah, Ezekiel and the Scroll of the Twelve Prophets.

[18] Outside of these, its occurrences are restricted to 2 Sam 5:7//1 Chr 11:5; 1 Kg 8:1//2 Chr 5:2; 2 Kg 19:21; 19:31; Song 3:11.

Given the frequent parallelism between Jerusalem and Zion,[19] the common perception is that the two names are simply different appellations of the same city, without any further connotation. However, as I repeatedly indicate in my commentaries, names are functional, especially when they refer to the same entity: Abram and Abraham, Sarai and Sarah, Simon and Peter, Saul and Paul. Jerusalem, whatever its supposed original, has to do with peace (*šalom*); this is made clear in scripture since, at one point, Jerusalem is referred to simply as Salem (*šalem*):[20] "In Judah God is known, his name is great in Israel. His abode has been established in Salem, his dwelling place in Zion." (Ps 76:1b-2) Of note is that the only other instance of Salem in the Old Testament occurs in Genesis 14:18. The king of Salem is Melchizedek [whose name means "My King is [my] righteousness,"] who "was priest of God Most High" and to whom even "Abram gave a tenth of everything" (v.20). Both Melchizedek and Salem enter the scene after Abram was able to save the people of Canaan by routing the four Kings from the east of the Euphrates. Since Genesis 14 is a self-standing chapter, unrelated to either what comes before or after it, Abram's feat is clearly intended as a prototype of the end of the Babylonian exile.[21] Such finds full corroboration in Jeremiah where the end of the exile is described in terms that underscore justice and righteousness just as in Isaiah 1:21-27; moreover both the new David and the new Jerusalem are dubbed "The Lord is our righteousness," which echoes Melchizedek:

---

[19] See, e.g., Is 2:3b (For out of Zion shall go forth the law, and the word of the Lord from Jerusalem).

[20] In Hebrew *šalom* is the noun (peace; sanity; wholesomeness) whereas *šalem* is the adjective (sane; wholesome; complete).

[21] Note that the chapter opens with the mention of "Amraphel king of Shinar." The two previous occurrences of Shinar (Gen 10:10; 11:2) clearly link it to Babel (10:10; 11:9).

Behold, the days are coming, says the Lord, when I will raise up for David a righteous Branch, and he shall reign as king and deal wisely, and shall execute justice (*mišpaṭ*) and righteousness (*ṣedaqah*) in the land. In his days Judah will be saved, and Israel will dwell securely. And this is the name by which he will be called: "The Lord is our righteousness (*ṣedeq*)." [22] (Jer 23:5-6)

In those days and at that time I will cause a righteous Branch to spring forth for David; and he shall execute justice (*mišpaṭ*) and righteousness (*ṣedaqah*) in the land. In those days Judah will be saved and Jerusalem will dwell securely. And this is the name by which it will be called: "The Lord is our righteousness (*ṣedeq*)." (33:15-16) JeRVSALEM

From all the preceding it is reasonable to conclude that the consonantal Hebrew *yerušalem* (Jerusalem) is constructed from the verb *yarah* (cast off, throw away), in its conjugated form *yaru* (they cast off; they throw away) and from the noun *šalem*, the resultant meaning being "they [the people] disregard the peace" granted by God. This inference is corroborated by the traditional reading of the original Hebrew as *yerušala[yi]m*.[23] The ending –*ayim* is rare; it is usually found in the words that denote dual human organs or limbs: eyes, ears, hands, feet. However, in certain names of locations, the dual form is used to underscore a connotation by doubling it. Two examples are *qarnayim* and *miṣrayim* (Egypt). In the case of *qarnayim*, whose literal meaning is "two horns"—a horn being a metaphor for strength or

---

[22] *ṣedeq* is the masculine form of the more common feminine *ṣedaqah*.

[23] Such has to be done through the otherwise unwarranted squeezing of the extra vowel *i* between the final consonants *l* and *m*. Technically speaking, this addition would have needed the additional consonant *y* to support the added vowel *i*. However, since inserting extra consonants would introduce a change in the Semitic consonantal text, it was prohibited out of deference to the sacredness of scripture.

power—the intent is to present a city as "double-horned" and thus difficult to conquer; consequently, conquering it would be a great feat worthy of pride: "But you have turned justice into poison and the fruit of righteousness into wormwood—you who rejoice in Lo-debar, who say, 'Have we not by our own strength taken Karnaim (*qarnayim*) for ourselves?' For behold, I will raise up against you a nation, O house of Israel, says the Lord, the God of hosts; and they shall oppress you from the entrance of Hamath to the Brook of the Arabah." (Am 6:12b-14) As for Egypt, the case is even more pertinent for our discussion since the scriptural *miṣrayim* is a made up Hebrew symbolic noun whose meaning is "from (out of) double (much) affliction."[24]

The intention of the forced construction of *yerušala[yi]m* actually finds support in scripture itself. First and foremost, the element "peace" in conjunction with Jerusalem and Judah is overarching in that, although time and again it has been refused by the people, God's ultimate goal is peace, and this will always be on his mind until he has implemented it: Jerusalem is *his* "city of peace" wherein the wicked and unrighteous will have no share:

O that you had hearkened to my commandments! Then your peace would have been like a river, and your righteousness like the waves of the sea; your offspring would have been like the sand, and your descendants like its grains; their name would never be cut off or destroyed from before me. Go forth from Babylon, flee from Chaldea, declare this with a shout of joy, proclaim it, send it forth to the end of the earth; say, "The Lord has redeemed his servant Jacob!" They thirsted not when he led them through the

---

[24] Our English "Egypt" is a transliteration of the Greek *Aigyptos* and the Ancient Egyptian hieroglyphic of that country is *Kemet*. Notice that the consonants of neither correspond to those of *miṣrayim*.

deserts; he made water flow for them from the rock; he cleft the rock and the water gushed out. "There is no peace," says the Lord, "for the wicked." (Is 48:18-22)

For the mountains may depart and the hills be removed, but my steadfast love shall not depart from you, and my covenant of peace shall not be removed, says the Lord, who has compassion on you. (54:10)

For as the rain and the snow come down from heaven, and return not thither but water the earth, making it bring forth and sprout, giving seed to the sower and bread to the eater, so shall my word be that goes forth from my mouth; it shall not return to me empty, but it shall accomplish that which I purpose, and prosper in the thing for which I sent it. For you shall go out in joy, and be led forth in peace; the mountains and the hills before you shall break forth into singing, and all the trees of the field shall clap their hands. (55:10-12)

The righteous man perishes, and no one lays it to heart; devout men are taken away, while no one understands. For the righteous man is taken away from calamity, he enters into peace; they rest in their beds who walk in their uprightness. (57:1-2)

The way of peace they know not, and there is no justice in their paths; they have made their roads crooked, no one who goes in them knows peace. (59:8)

Instead of bronze I will bring gold, and instead of iron I will bring silver; instead of wood, bronze, instead of stones, iron. I will make your overseers peace and your taskmasters righteousness. (60:17)

Then I said: "Ah, Lord God, behold, the prophets say to them, 'You shall not see the sword, nor shall you have famine, but I will give you assured peace in this place.'" (Jer 14:13)

What is striking, however, is that one can also find support for the choice of the dual ending in the passages where an intended aural stress on the importance of "peace" is reflected in the repetition of that word:

> In that day: "A pleasant vineyard, sing of it! I, the Lord, am its keeper; every moment I water it. Lest any one harm it, I guard it night and day; I have no wrath. Would that I had thorns and briers to battle! I would set out against them, I would burn them up together. Or let them lay hold of my protection, let them make peace with me, let them make peace with me." (Is 27:2-5)

> Peace, peace, to the far and to the near, says the Lord; and I will heal him. But the wicked are like the tossing sea; for it cannot rest, and its waters toss up mire and dirt. There is no peace, says my God, for the wicked. (57:19-21)

> They have healed the wound of my people lightly, saying, "Peace, peace," when there is no peace. (Jer 6:14; 8:11)

Zion

The Hebrew *ṣiyyon* is from the same root as the verb *ṣiwwah* (command), whence *miṣwah* (commandment). Consequently Zion would be the "city of the Law" when compared to Jerusalem, the "city of peace." Since peace is contingent on justice and righteousness, which are secured to the extent that the leaders and the people alike abide by the commandments of the Law, one would expect to find indications in scripture that, functionally speaking, Zion has a higher value than Jerusalem. A quick overview of scripture will confirm such an expectation.

The first instance of Zion occurs in 2 Samuel in conjunction with "the city of David." More specifically, we are told that, after "having taken the stronghold of Zion" (5:7), David "dwelt in the stronghold, and called it the city of David" (v.9). However, this action takes place after the following statement: "And David said on that day, 'Whoever would smite the Jebusites, let him get up the water shaft to attack the lame and the blind, who are hated by David's soul.' Therefore it is said, 'The blind and the lame shall not come into the house.'" (v.8) Put otherwise, David transformed Zion, the city of the Lord who rules there through his Law, into his own personal possession and established his own ruling which excised out of that city the lame and the blind. The patient hearer of scripture will discover in the Latter Prophets that God himself will welcome both the lame and the blind in the restored Zion.[25]

There is further evidence that David intended to impose his total control on Zion. In spite of his appearance of submission to the ark of the covenant containing the Law, he actually did so on his own terms and solely for his own profit. It is worthwhile to hear the entire passage with all the details concerning this matter:

David again gathered all the chosen men of Israel, thirty thousand. And David arose and went with all the people who were with him from Baalejudah, to bring up from there the ark of God, which is called by the name of the Lord of hosts who sits enthroned on the cherubim. And they carried the ark of God upon a new cart, and brought it out of the house of Abinadab which was on the hill; and Uzzah and Ahio, the sons of Abinadab, were driving the new cart with the ark of God; and Ahio went before the ark. And David and all the house of Israel were making merry before the Lord with all their might, with songs and lyres and harps and tambourines and castanets and cymbals. And when they came to the threshing floor of Nacon, Uzzah put out his hand to the ark of God and took hold of it, for the oxen stumbled. And the anger of

---

[25] Is 29:18; 33:23; 35:5-6; 42:16; Jer 31:8; Mic 4:6-7; Zeph 3:19.

the Lord was kindled against Uzzah; and God smote him there because he put forth his hand to the ark; and he died there beside the ark of God. And David was angry because the Lord had broken forth (*paraṣ*) upon Uzzah (*'uzzah*); and that place is called Perezuzzah (*pereṣ 'uzzah*), to this day. And David was afraid of the Lord that day; and he said, "How can the ark of the Lord come to me?" So David was not willing to take the ark of the Lord into the city of David; but David took it aside to the house of Obededom the Gittite. And the ark of the Lord remained in the house of Obededom the Gittite three months; and the Lord blessed Obededom and all his household. And it was told King David, "The Lord has blessed the household of Obededom and all that belongs to him, because of the ark of God." So David went and brought up the ark of God from the house of Obededom to the city of David with rejoicing; and when those who bore the ark of the Lord had gone six paces, he sacrificed an ox and a fatling. And David danced before the Lord with all his might; and David was girded with a linen ephod. So David and all the house of Israel brought up the ark of the Lord with shouting, and with the sound of the horn. (2 Sam 6:1-15)

Later, the attitude of David will be corrected under his son, Solomon, when the ark of the covenant will be "brought up" ceremoniously "*out of* the city of David, which is Zion" (1 Kg 8:1) into its new official residence, built specifically for that purpose. What earlier was "Zion, that is, the city of David" (2 Sam 5:7) is now "the city of David, which is Zion."[26] Zion is reestablished as the city of God and his Law as reflected in Solomon's prayer (1 Kings 8:33-40) that refers back to the conditions of the Law (Deut 28:15-68). The irony is that Solomon was not aware that he would end as miserably as his father David (1Kings 11:1-13), precipitating centuries of total

---

[26] The Hebrew for "that is" and "which is" is the same *hi'*.

[handwritten marginalia at top:] Zion = the city of Law (or of righteousness by obedience to God). Jerusalem = the city of peace, but the peace was cast away by the peoples' disregard of God's law

disregard for the Law's statutes and ordinances by kings and people alike, which would bring about the implementation of that Law's curses (2 Kg 24-25). This is why in Isaiah 1 it is precisely Zion, the city of God that was supposed to be a faithful city, full of justice and righteousness, which the four kings (Is 1) of "the house of David" (7:2, 13) and his "sons" (38:5) are accused of turning into a "harlot" (1:21). However, this time around, it is not Solomon who will redress the situation (1 Kg 8:1), but the Lord of hosts himself:

> Therefore the Lord says, the Lord of hosts, the Mighty One of Israel: "Ah, I will vent my wrath on my enemies, and avenge myself on my foes. I will turn my hand against you and will smelt away your dross as with lye and remove all your alloy. And I will restore your judges as at the first, and your counselors as at the beginning. Afterward you shall be called the city of righteousness, the faithful city." (Is 1:24-26)

The unevenness between Zion and Jerusalem, in spite of their frequent overlapping, can be detected in passages where Zion is presented more so as God's "heavenly" abode and Jerusalem more so as his "earthly" temple erected by human hand. An overview of their occurrences in Psalms, the liturgical book of God's temple, will readily show such differentiation.

- In Book I (Ps 1-41) the hearers are overwhelmed with five mentions of Zion (Ps 2:6; 9:11, 14; 14:7; 20:2) and the total absence of Jerusalem; the tone of the Book of Psalms is set: God's "holy hill" (2:6) where he "dwells" (9:11) and whence "deliverance for Israel would come" (14:7), and his "sanctuary" whence "he sends help" and "gives support" (20:2) is unequivocally Zion.

- In Book II (Ps 42-72), Jerusalem is brought timidly into the picture so that the hearers would realize that it is simply an earthly city for earthly kings to visit and bring gifts to God (68:29). Being such, it is always threatened with destruction like any other city and thus its walls have to be "rebuilt" (51:18). Even so, Jerusalem is eclipsed by the controlling "presence" of Zion (48:2, 11, 12; 50:2; 51:18; 53:6; 65:1; 69:35). Moreover, in its first mention Jerusalem is just an echo of that of Zion, as though it is under the umbrage of Zion: "Do good to Zion in thy good pleasure; rebuild the walls of Jerusalem." (51:18) The rebuilding of Jerusalem's walls is contingent upon the repentance of David, the king who wanted to subdue Zion to his own will (2 Sam 5-6). In order not to leave any shred of doubt as to his intentions, the author carefully squeezes reference to Jerusalem as the earthly location of the temple (68:29) between two mentions of Zion (Ps 65:1; 69:35). The first mention preempts any misunderstanding of 68:29 by having David himself, who will sing "the song" of Psalm 68, already state that the true place of worship is Zion: "To the choirmaster. A Psalm of David. A Song. Praise is due to thee, O God, in Zion; and to thee shall vows be performed" (65:1); "To the choirmaster. A Psalm of David. A Song. Let God arise, let his enemies be scattered; let those who hate him flee before him!" (68:1) The second mention of Zion (69:35) makes sure to underscore the secondary status of Jerusalem compared to that of Zion. Although the walls of Jerusalem will be rebuilt, it is not she, but Zion that will be the "capital" of restored Judah: "For God will save Zion and rebuild the cities of Judah; and his servants shall dwell there and possess it; the children of his servants shall inherit it, and those who love his name shall dwell in it." (69:35-36)

- The pattern encountered in Book II is found again in the short Book III (Ps 73-89). It is only in Psalm 79 that we hear twice of Jerusalem, and no less in ruin (vv.1 and 3). Surrounding these verses is a formidable array of statements where Zion is hailed with the highest possible praises:

> Remember thy congregation, which thou hast gotten of old, which thou hast redeemed to be the tribe of thy heritage! Remember Mount Zion, where thou hast dwelt. (74:2)

> His abode has been established in Salem, his dwelling place in Zion.[27] (76:2)

> But he chose the tribe of Judah, Mount Zion, which he loves.[28] (78:68)

> Blessed are the men whose strength is in thee, in whose heart are the [right] ways[29] ... They go from strength to strength; the God of gods will be seen in Zion. (84:5, 7)

> The Lord loves the gates of Zion more than all the dwelling places of Jacob. (87:2)

> And of Zion it shall be said, "This one and that one were born in her"; for the Most High himself will establish her. (87:5)

---

[27] Notice how, at equating Jerusalem with Zion as God's abode, the author purposely used the name Salem.

[28] Notice the full equation of the tribe of Judah with Mount Zion, its "capital," rather than with Jerusalem.

[29] RSV has "the highways to Zion."

- In the following and equally short Book IV we have five references to Zion (97:8; 99:2; 102:13, 16, 21). In the last reference, Jerusalem is fully equated with Zion:

> Thou wilt arise and have pity on Zion; it is the time to favor her; the appointed time has come. For thy servants hold her stones dear, and have pity on her dust. The nations will fear the name of the Lord, and all the kings of the earth thy glory. For the Lord will build up Zion, he will appear in his glory; he will regard the prayer of the destitute, and will not despise their supplication. Let this be recorded for a generation to come, so that a people yet unborn may praise the Lord: that he looked down from his holy height, from heaven the Lord looked at the earth, to hear the groans of the prisoners, to set free those who were doomed to die; that men may declare in Zion the name of the Lord, and in Jerusalem his praise, when peoples gather together, and kingdoms, to worship the Lord. (102:13-22)

Since the passage speaks of a time of favor (v.13), when prisoners are set free (v.20), and peoples and kingdoms (v.22) as well as nations and kings (v.15) join in beholding God's glory in Zion—terminology which is found in Isaiah 40-66—one gets the distinct impression that the background is the return from the Babylonian exile, especially that the two immediately preceding instances of Jerusalem in Book III refer to its being in ruins (Ps 79:1, 3). The impression becomes certitude when one considers that Psalm 90, which opens Book IV, is the only psalm in the Psalter ascribed to Moses, the exodus leader, who is beseeching God to "return and have pity on your servants" (v.13) who suffered his wrath for their sins (vv.7-8). This again is terminology reminiscent of Isaiah 40-66 that depicts the return from Babylon in terms of the exodus from Egypt (43:2, 16; 51:10) and the journey in the wilderness (40:3; 43:20; 48:21). In fact, the only instance where Moses is mentioned by name in Isaiah occurs in reference to the exodus: "Then he remembered the days of old, of Moses his servant. Where is he who brought up out of the sea the shepherds of his flock? Where is he who put in the midst of them his holy Spirit, who caused his glorious arm to go at the right hand of Moses, who divided the waters before them to make for himself an everlasting name, who led them through the depths? Like a horse in the desert, they did not stumble." (63:11-13) The conclusion is unmistakable: Jerusalem becomes Zion-like only after it is redeemed.

- In the lengthy Book V (Ps 106-150), which contains both the series of *hallel* (praise) Psalms (107, 111-118, 135-136, 146-150) and the "Psalms of Ascent" sandwiched in between (120-134), Zion and Jerusalem are mentioned nearly the same number of times—Zion tops Jerusalem only fourteen to twelve. Still, just as it enjoyed the exclusive place of honor in Book I, it is Zion that has the last word in the entire Psalter. After its joining with Jerusalem in 147:12, where Jerusalem is even granted priority (Praise the Lord, O Jerusalem! Praise your God, O Zion!),[30] it is Zion alone that fills the scene at the end: "Praise the Lord! Sing to the Lord a new song, his praise in the assembly of the faithful! Let Israel be glad in his Maker, let the sons of Zion rejoice in

---

[30] Until then it is Zion that has the priority (51:18; 125:1-2; 128:5; 135:21; 137:1, 3, and 5, 6, 7).

their King!" (149:1-2) A closer look will show that this
sequence is actually a set up. Psalm 147 is dedicated to
the building up of Jerusalem (v.2), and it is in her
renewed state that she becomes Zion, which in turn is
hailed as the city of the omnipotent King and Maker of
Israel (149:2).

This reading of Zion (*ṣiyyon*) as the city of the non-iconic God
whose visible presence is reflected exclusively in the
commandments (*miṣwot*) of his law (*torah*) is corroborated in the
structure of the Book of Psalms. The Psalter opens with two
untitled psalms that function as an introduction to the entire
Psalter. Before they encounter Zion, the Lord's "holy hill," for the
first time in Psalm 2:6, the hearers have already been programmed
to understand that this Lord has been revealed in the Book of the
Law: "Blessed is the man (*'ašre ha'iš*) who walks not in the counsel
of the wicked, nor stands in the way of sinners, nor sits in the seat
of scoffers; but his delight is in the law (*torah*) of the Lord, and on
his law he meditates[31] day and night." (1:2) That these two psalms
are meant to be read in tandem is evident in that the conclusion of
Psalm 2 corresponds to the opening of Psalm 1: "Blessed are all
(*'ašre kol*) who take refuge in him." (Ps 2:11c) In other words,
Zion, beginning with its earthly king, is made of human beings
who obediently follow the dictates of the Law.

---

[31] The original Hebrew means "and his law he mumbles (by heart)." See *C-Josh* 77-78.

Chapter 2
Why the Call of the Prophet?

With the exception of Amos, whenever a prophetic book contains the classic "call of the prophet" passage, it is found right at the start of the book (Jer; Ezek; Hos; Jon). Nevertheless, in all prophetic books, including Amos, precedence is given to the prophet's "words" rather than to his person or to the manner in which he was called. This is confirmed in the many other prophetic books where there is no reference at all to the "call" (Joel; Ob; Mic; Nah; Hab; Zeph; Hag; Zech; Mal). The uniqueness of Isaiah is that the "call" takes place later in the Isaianic story (ch 6). It is as though the author wanted the hearers to be convinced of the validity of God's decision to "raise" a prophet who would carry the divine message. To be sure, within the other books the hearers learn the valid reason for the prophet's call; however, since Isaiah is positioned as the first book of the latter Prophets, it is important and fitting to immediately overwhelm the hearers with the "sin" of Judah, described over four chapters (Is 2-5), so that by end of the lengthy invective they would not only be expecting the extreme harshness of the divine verdict, but also be ready to fully endorse it:

> And he [the Lord] said, "Go, and say to this people: 'Hear and hear, but do not understand; see and see, but do not perceive.' Make the heart of this people fat, and their ears heavy, and shut their eyes; lest they see with their eyes, and hear with their ears, and understand with their hearts, and turn and be healed." Then I said, "How long, O Lord?" And he said: "Until cities lie waste without inhabitant, and houses without men, and the land is

utterly desolate, and the Lord removes men far away, and the forsaken places are many in the midst of the land. And though a tenth remain in it, it will be burned again, like a terebinth or an oak, whose stump remains standing when it is felled." (6:9-13)

Accordingly, when hearing the call of Jeremiah (1:11-18) in the next prophetic book, they would have already been primed and would not question the Lord's decision.

After the introductory chapter to the entire tripartite book, the indictment against Jerusalem and Judah (Is 2-5) opens with a liturgical hymn in praise of the Lord's mountain (2:2-4), which is primarily introduced as Zion:

> [2]It shall come to pass in the latter days that the mountain of the house of the Lord shall be established as the highest of the mountains, and shall be raised about hills; and all the nations shall flow to it, [3]and many peoples shall come, and say: "Come, let us to up to the mountain of the Lord, to the house of the God of Jacob; that he may teach us his ways and that we may walk in his paths." For out of Zion shall go forth the law, and the word of the Lord from Jerusalem. [4]He shall judge (šapaṭ) between the nations, and shall decide (hokiaḥ; from the verb yakaḥ) for many peoples; and they shall beat their swords into plowshares, and their spears into pruning hooks; nation shall not lift up sword against nation, neither shall they learn war any more. (vv.2-4)[1]

The primacy of Zion over Jerusalem is evident in that what comes forth out of Zion and also out from Jerusalem is God's law and teaching which are elements connected with Zion.[2] To be sure, the peace reflected in the name Jerusalem is underscored in v.4b;

---

[1] Such finds corroboration in Psalms where it is always Zion, and never Jerusalem, that is connected with the mount(ain) of God (48:2; 74:2; 87:1; 99:1-2, 9).
[2] See my discussion of Zion in the previous chapter.

however, that peace is the result of God emitting his just judgment (*mišpaṭ*) among all nations (v.4a). It is the verb *yakaḥ* that is used to describe God's intervention to redress the disastrous situation brought about by the people's disobedience. This intervention in turn required the same people to submit to God's will:

> Come now, let us reason together (*niwwakeḥah*), says the Lord: though your sins are like scarlet, they shall be as white as snow; though they are red like crimson, they shall become like wool. If you are willing and obedient, you shall eat the good of the land; but if you refuse and rebel, you shall be devoured by the sword; for the mouth of the Lord has spoken. (1:18-20)

Thus Zion will be restored to being the "faithful city" only insomuch as its citizens abide by the Law. Still, what is new in Isaiah 2:2-4, when compared to chapter 1, is that the peace enacted through submission to the Law is universal; it encompasses not only the "house of Jacob" (2:5) but the "nations" as well (vv.2b-3). Conveying God's law to the nations will be the express mission of the Lord's chosen "servant" (Is 42:1-7; 49:1-6), with the outcome being that "the foreigners who join themselves to the Lord, to minister to him, to love the name of the Lord, and to be his servants, every one who keeps the sabbath, and does not profane it, and holds fast my covenant—these I will bring to my holy mountain, and make them joyful in my house of prayer; their burnt offerings and their sacrifices will be accepted on my altar; for my house shall be called a house of prayer for all peoples" (56:6-7). So the hymn of 2:2-4, which mentions both "the mountain of the Lord" and "the house of the God of Jacob" (v.3) as well as combines them into "the mountain of the house of the Lord" (v.2), and which opens with the words "It shall come to pass in the latter days," unmistakably looks ahead to the new Zion described later in the

book (56-66). In other words, the hymn describes the restored
Zion, Zion as it should have been: the holy mountain where
God dwells and issues his "statutes and ordinances" so that the
house of Jacob can walk in their light (2:5), that is to say, "be
careful to do them" (Deut 5:1; 6:3; 26:16; 28:13).
Unfortunately, the house of Jacob disobeyed the Law (Is 2:6-22)
and forced God to devise his lengthy "Isaianic" plan in order to
reestablish his city Zion, which is the subject matter of the Book
of Isaiah.

For the time being, the order of the day, as we already heard in
chapter 1, is the punishment of Judah and in a most extreme
manner, no less: "For thou hast rejected (*naṭaštah*; from the verb
verb *naṭaš*) thy people, the house of Jacob." (2:6a) The hearer
must not be scandalized that God's interest lies in his holy
mountain Zion where he dwells. All the other "human"
dwellings raised for him by Israel are only transitory as we learn
from Psalm 78:60 and also from Jeremiah (6:12-14; 26:6-9)
where we hear of Shiloh, the first locale for the tent of meeting
in the earth of Canaan. It is "before the Lord in Shiloh" that the
inheritances were allocated to the tribes:

> Then the whole congregation of the people of Israel assembled at
> Shiloh,[3] and set up the tent of meeting there ... So the men
> started on their way; and Joshua charged those who went to write
> the description of the land, saying, "Go up and down and write a
> description of the land, and come again to me; and I will cast lots
> for you here before the Lord in Shiloh." So the men went and
> passed up and down in the land and set down in a book a
> description of it by towns in seven divisions; then they came to
> Joshua in the camp at Shiloh, and Joshua cast lots for them in

---

[3] This is the first instance of Shiloh in scripture.

Shiloh before the Lord; and there Joshua apportioned the land to the people of Israel, to each his portion. (Josh 18:1, 8-10)

And yet it is made clear in Psalm 78 that Shiloh is just as a transient stop for the Lord on the way to his dwelling, Zion:

And he brought them to his holy land, to the mountain which his right hand had won. He drove out nations before them; he apportioned them for a possession and settled the tribes of Israel in their tents. Yet they tested and rebelled against the Most High God, and did not observe his testimonies, but turned away and acted treacherously like their fathers; they twisted like a deceitful bow. For they provoked him to anger with their high places; they moved him to jealousy with their graven images. When God heard, he was full of wrath, and he utterly rejected Israel. He forsook (rejected; *yiṭṭoš* from the verb *naṭaš*) his dwelling at Shiloh, the tent where he dwelt among men ... He rejected the tent of Joseph, he did not choose the tribe of Ephraim; but he chose the tribe of Judah, Mount Zion, which he loves. He built his sanctuary like the high heavens, like the earth, which he has founded for ever. (vv. 54-60, 67-69)

The inhabitants of Jerusalem and Judah erred in thinking that the temple they built for the Lord in Jerusalem would supplant Shiloh for good. They considered *their* Jerusalem temple tantamount to the Lord's dwelling, Zion. However, when they kept committing the same sins as those who resided around Shiloh, the same Lord sent them a double wakeup call, reminding them that Jerusalem has no higher intrinsic value than Shiloh:

For if you truly amend your ways and your doings, if you truly execute justice one with another, if you do not oppress the alien, the fatherless or the widow, or shed innocent blood in this place, and if you do not go after other gods to your own hurt, then I will let you dwell in this place, in the land that I gave of old to your fathers for ever. Behold, you trust in deceptive words to no avail. Will you steal, murder, commit adultery, swear falsely, burn incense to Baal, and go after other gods that you have not known, and then come and stand before me in this house, which is called by my name, and say, "We are delivered!"— only to go on doing all these abominations? Has this house, which is called by my name, become a den of robbers in your eyes? Behold, I myself have seen it, says the Lord. Go now to my place that was in Shiloh, where I made my name dwell at first, and see what I did to it for the wickedness of my people Israel. And now, because you have done all these things, says the Lord, and when I spoke to you persistently you did not listen, and when I called you, you did not answer, therefore I will do to the house which is called by my name, and in which you trust, and to the place which I gave to you and to your fathers, as I did to Shiloh. (Jer 7:5-14)

Thus says the Lord: "If you will not listen to me, to walk in my law which I have set before you, and to heed the words of my servants the prophets whom I send to you urgently, though you have not heeded, then I will make this house like Shiloh, and I will make this city a curse for all the nations of the earth." The priests and the prophets and all the people heard Jeremiah speaking these words in the house of the Lord. And when Jeremiah had finished speaking all that the Lord had commanded him to speak to all the people, then the priests and the prophets and all the people laid hold of him, saying, "You shall die! Why have you prophesied in the name of the Lord, saying, 'This house shall be like Shiloh, and this city shall be desolate, without inhabitant'?" (26:4-9)

The obstinacy of the leaders and people will eventually lead to the demise of Jerusalem and its temple at the hand of the Babylonians. That the rejection mentioned in Isaiah 2:6a has in view the rejection of Jerusalem is corroborated in the first part of

Isaiah (2-39) that closes with the prophet's words: "Hear the word of the Lord of hosts: Behold, the days are coming, when all that is in your house, and that which your fathers have stored up till this day, shall be carried to Babylon; nothing shall be left, says the Lord. And some of your own sons, who are born to you, shall be taken away; and they shall be eunuchs in the palace of the king of Babylon." (39:5-7)

For our ears, trained into classical theology that tends to sugarcoat God, especially in his dealings with us, the most striking feature of God in the message of the prophets is the outright equivalence between his terror and the glory (radiance) of his majesty. Most probably this was striking even to the prophet's contemporaries who tended to equate God's coming to them as "a day of light and brightness." Such a thought was so engrained in them that the Lord needed to assign Amos to declare to Israel:

> Woe to you who desire the day of the Lord! Why would you have the day of the Lord? It is darkness, and not light; as if a man fled from a lion, and a bear met him; or went into the house and leaned with his hand against the wall, and a serpent bit him. Is not the day of the Lord darkness, and not light, and gloom with no brightness in it? (5:18-20)

Isaiah had to state thrice that God's punishing terror was nothing other than the radiance of his majesty (2:10, 19, 21). This will be further evident in the "call of Isaiah" when upon beholding God's glory filling the whole earth, the prophet exclaims: "Woe is me!" (6:5)   *↑ the glory of His might*

The parallelism between Amos 5 and Isaiah 2 is secured through the reference to "the day of the Lord (of hosts)" (Is 2:12). However, "the day of the Lord" is always associated with judgment. Anyone familiar with the Ancient Near East will know that a deity's "office" is to judge, and the supreme deity is judge of all, gods and humans alike:[4]

> A Psalm of Asaph. God has taken his place in the divine council; in the midst of the gods he holds judgment: "How long will you judge unjustly and show partiality to the wicked? Give justice to the weak and the fatherless; maintain the right of the afflicted and the destitute. Rescue the weak and the needy; deliver them from the hand of the wicked." They have neither knowledge nor understanding, they walk about in darkness; all the foundations of the earth are shaken. I say, "You are gods, sons of the Most High, all of you; nevertheless, you shall die like men, and fall like any prince." Arise, O God, judge the earth; for to thee belong all the nations! (Ps 82:1-8)

This is just what one hears in Isaiah 2 where God judges both man (v.9) and the other deities (v.18) that man honors (v.8).

The sin aimed at in vv.12-16 is the arrogance of the powerful human beings as is evident in the examples used as well as by the vocabulary itself:

> For the Lord of hosts has a day against all that is proud and lofty, against all that is lifted up and high, against all the cedars of Lebanon, lofty and lifted up; and against all the oaks of Bashan; against all the high mountains, and against all the lofty hills; against every high tower, and against every fortified wall; against all the ships of Tarshish, and against all the beautiful craft.

However, the arrogance signified is not a "vice," that is to say, something essentially bad or evil per se. Rather, it is to emphasize

---

[4] This reality is reflected in the Arabic language of the *qur'an* where the same word *din* is used to connote "judgment" as well as "religion." The corollary is that the God that is honored in religion is essentially judge.

that "haughtiness" befits God and him alone. In other words, the human being, in whose "nostrils" is mere "breath" (v.22), is ultimately as breakable clay (Gen 2:7);[5] it is only insofar and insomuch as he wants to "play" god, if not take God's place, that his haughtiness is *peša'*, a revolt against the bestower of life and all good things. This supposition is supported by the text itself:

> The haughty looks of man (*'adam*) shall be brought low, and the pride (*rum*) of men shall be humbled; and the Lord alone will be exalted in that day. For the Lord of hosts has a day against all that is proud and lofty (*ram*), against all that is lifted up (*nišša'*), which shall be brought low[6]... And the haughtiness of man (*ha'adam*) shall be humbled, and the pride (*rum*) of men shall be brought low; and the Lord alone will be exalted in that day. (vv.11-12, 17)

The hearers will be reminded of that a few chapters later when Isaiah will be called to deliver the message of punishment by "the Lord sitting upon a throne, high (*ram*) and lifted up (*nišša'*)" (6:1). And the nations better beware since they are also included in the message (2:2-4) that is addressed beyond "the house of Jacob" (v.6), to every human being (*'adam*; vv.11, 17), even those who will end up hiding in caverns with Israel:

> In that day men (*ha'adam*; the human being in general, every human being) will cast forth their idols of silver and their idols of gold, which they made for themselves to worship, to the moles and to the bats, to enter the caverns of the rocks and the clefts of the cliffs, from before the terror of the Lord, and from the glory of his majesty, when he rises to terrify the earth. (vv.20-21)

---

[5] "then the Lord God formed man of dust from the ground, and breathed into his nostrils the breath of life; and man became a living being."

[6] RSV has incorrectly "against all that is lifted up and high."

Psalm 130 (131)

The last summons to *all* the human beings is to turn away from any man, especially the one filled with one's unwarranted hubris: "Turn away (*ḥidlu*; imperative plural) from man (*ha'adam*) in whose nostrils is breath." (v.22a) It is as though the message is to turn away from one's *own* haughtiness. This literary irony is used to trap the hearers, and it will be used again in chapter 5.

Isaiah 3:1-4:1 goes into detail to cover the severe punishment the Lord is leveling against both the rich and powerful men (3:1-13) and their wives who exploit their husbands' richness (3:16-4:1; see also Am 4:1-3).

> 3:12My people—children are their oppressors, and women rule over them, O my people, your leaders mislead you, and confuse the course of your paths. 13The Lord has taken his place to contend, he stands to judge his people. 14The Lord enters into judgment with the elders and princes of his people; "It is you who have devoured the vineyard, the spoil of the poor is in your houses. 15What do you mean by crushing my people, by grinding the face of the poor?" says the Lord God of hosts. 16The Lord said: Because the daughters of Zion are haughty and walk with outstretched necks, glancing wantonly with their eyes, mincing along as they go, tinkling with their feet; 17the Lord will smite with a scab the heads of the daughters of Zion and the Lord will lay bare their secret parts.

Their sin lies in taking advantage of the poor and needy (3:12, 15; see earlier 1:6) who are referred to by God as "my people." However, in preparation for the indictment of chapter 5, these are also introduced as his "vineyard" (*kerem*) in 13:14.

Given the oppressiveness of chapters 2 and 3, before proceeding with the indictment against the leaders of Jerusalem and Judah (ch.5), the author goes on a tangent that gives hope for the future to the "remnant" he referred to in 1:9: "If the Lord of hosts had not left (*hotir*, from the verb *yatar*) us a few survivors, we should have been like Sodom, and become like Gomorrah." In chapter 4 he addresses his hearers, who were just overwhelmed by the content of chapters 2 and 3, and are assumedly vegetating either in exile or in devastated Jerusalem, as that remnant:

Very different from orthodox SB:

> [4:2] In that day the branch (*ṣemaḥ*; sprout) of the Lord shall be beautiful and glorious, and the fruit of the land shall be the pride and glory of the survivors (*pheleṭah*; escapees) of Israel. [3] And he who is left (*niš'ar*, from the verb *ša'ar* and the same root as the noun *še'ar* [rest, remainder]) in Zion and remains (*notar*, from the verb *yatar*) in Jerusalem will be called holy, every one who has been recorded for life in Jerusalem, [4] when the Lord shall have washed away the filth of the daughters of Zion and cleansed the bloodstains of Jerusalem from its midst by a spirit of judgment and by a spirit of burning. [5] Then the Lord will create (*bara'*) over the whole site of Mount Zion and over her assemblies a cloud by day, and smoke and the shining of a flaming fire by night; for over all the glory there will be a canopy and a pavilion. [6] It will be for a shade by day from the heat, and for a refuge and a shelter from the storm and rain.

That the author has in mind the hope for a post-exilic restoration is evident in that, in addition to our passage, the root *ṣmḥ* in the verbal form *ṣamaḥ* (sprout) occurs seven times in chapters 40-66 which speak about that restoration. Similarly, except for its instance in 4:5, the verb *bara'* (create) is a trademark of those same chapters where it is found no less than twenty times. Moreover, the view that the restored Zion will be a pavilion under a canopy, similar to the tent of meeting in the wilderness, is also underscored in chapter 66 where the Lord says: "Heaven is my throne and the earth is my footstool; what is the house which you would build for me, and what is the place of my rest? All these things my hand has made, and so all these things are mine." (vv.1-2)

Another feature of Isaiah 4:2-6 is that, while referring to the root *ntr* which occurred in 1:9 to speak of the "remainder" of survivors, it introduces as its parallel in meaning the root *š'r* which will occupy the center stage in chapters 7-12[7] and all those instances, as we shall see, concern Samaria and the kingdom of Israel rather than Jerusalem and the kingdom of Judah. The obvious intention is to include into the restored congregation of the new Zion not only the Judahite exiles in Babylon but also the Ephraimite exiles in Assyria. This is a recurrent theme in the Latter Prophets.[8]

The Lord's Vineyard

The most powerful passage of chapters 2-5 is the lawsuit of God against his people (5:1-7) that begins with the eloquent "song of the vineyard" (vv.1-2).[9] The forcefulness of the poem lies in the fact that the clue to its true intent is given in the last word *be'ushim* (wild, i.e., worthless, grapes) in v.2:

> [1]Let me sing for my beloved a love song concerning his vineyard. My beloved had a vineyard on a very fertile hill. [2]He digged it and cleared it of stones, and planted it with choice vines; he built a watchtower in the midst of it, and hewed out a wine vat in it; and he looked for it to yield grapes, but it yielded wild grapes. [3]And now, O inhabitants of Jerusalem and men of Judah, judge I pray you between me and my vineyard. [4]What more was there to do for my vineyard, that I have not done in it? When I looked for it to

---

[7] Ten instances in the Hebrew original (7:3; 10:19, 20, 21 [twice], 22; 11:11 [twice], 16 [twice]) compared to only one *notar* in 7:22.

[8] Is 11:12; Jer 3:6-13, 17; Ezek 23:1-49; 37:15-28: Hos 1:10-11.

[9] This was taken over by Jesus in his parable of the wicked husbandmen (Mt 21:33-46//Mk 12:1-12//Lk 20:9-19).

yield grapes, why did it yield wild grapes? [5]And now I will tell you
what I will do to my vineyard. I will remove its hedge, and it shall
be devoured; I will break down its wall, and it shall be trampled
down. [6]I will make it a waste; it shall not be pruned or hoed, and
briers and thorns shall grow up; I will command the clouds that
they rain no rain upon it. [7]For the vineyard of the Lord of hosts is
the house of Israel, and the men of Judah are his pleasant planting;
and he looked for justice, but behold, bloodshed; for
righteousness, but behold, a cry!

The entire poem is designed to draw the hearers into expecting a
positive result to the hard and careful work of the
husbandman—and then suddenly without warning it springs a
negative surprise upon them. The prophets often use such a
literary device. Indeed, how could the Judahites who listened to
it, and who were naturally familiar with the difficult life of
agriculture, disagree that this must have been a worthless
vineyard to give such poor return after such diligent care (vv.3-
6)? Then, just as they are thinking to themselves something like
"put that vineyard to the torch," again comes a surprise: they
themselves are the vineyard (v.7)! But by now it is too late to
back down, for they have already acknowledged the justice of
God's indictment. All that remains is to await his sentence. So
now the time is ripe for the Lord to choose and send out his
messenger (ch.6). The call of the prophet in chapter 6 is the
culmination toward which chapter 5 leads. This is confirmed on
a formal literary level. The indictment in chapter 5 consists of six
"woes":

Woe to those who join house to house, who add field to field,
until there is no more room, and you are made to dwell along in
the midst of the land. (v.8)

Woe to those who rise early in the morning, that they may run after strong drink, who tarry late into the evening till the wine inflames them! (v.11)

Woe to those who draw iniquity with cords of falsehood, who draw sin as with cart ropes. (v.18)

Woe to those who call evil good and good evil, who put darkness for light and light for darkness, who put bitter for sweet and sweet for bitter! (v.20)

Woe to those who are wise in their own eyes and shrew in their own sight! (v.21)

Woe to those who are heroes at drinking wine, and valiant men in mixing strong drink. (v.22)

These woes prepare for the seventh and consummate "woe" on the lips of Isaiah himself in chapter 6 (v.5).[10] Isaiah's endorsement of God's verdict makes him ready to accept the difficult mission of announcing the divine indictment against Jerusalem and Judah.

---

[10] The next "woe" does not occur until 10:1.

Chapter 3
The Call of Isaiah   *Isaiah 6*

Although kingship is dynastic, people of Ancient Near Eastern kingdoms considered their reigning monarch to be the son of the deity in the sense that he was its direct representative.[1] This fact made the person of the king the basis for order, prosperity, and life within his realm.[2] Hence the belief that the absence of a king at any point in time was inconceivable; this belief later gave rise to the traditional proclamation "The king is dead; long live the king!" The herald who announces the death of the king declares *at the same time* the heir as king. The anticipation of the coronation and enthronement secures the continuous presence of the king within the kingdom, thus ensuring that it does not, even for a moment, lose its basis for existence and fall prey to chaos and destruction. Given such a view of kingship, one can imagine how alarming Uzziah's leprosy (2 Kg 15:5a) must have been to his Judahite subjects, especially since this sickness "eats away" the body and in so doing gradually destroys the person himself. In Uzziah's case his weakness was such that his son Jotham had to administer the kingdom as his regent while Uzziah himself remained confined to his quarters (2 Kg 15:5b).

Isaiah considered Uzziah's state of health a reflection of the bankruptcy of the Judahite kingship itself. Therefore when Uzziah died, Isaiah did not recognize the accession of Jotham as the solution to the problem. The only possible answer in his eyes

---

[1] See 2 Sam 7:12-16; Ps 2; 89:26.
[2] See Ps 72.

was for the Lord himself to take over the reins of kingship, and this is precisely the theme of chapter 6.

> [1]In the year that King Uzziah died I saw the Lord sitting upon a throne, high and lifted up; and his train filled the temple. [2]Above him stood the seraphim; each had six wings: with two he covered his face and with two he covered his feet, and with two he flew. [3]And one called to another and said: "Holy, holy, holy is the Lord of hosts; the whole earth is full of his glory." [4]And the foundations of the thresholds shook at the voice of him who called, and the house was filled with smoke. [5]And I said: "Woe is me! For I am lost; for I am a man of unclean lips, and I dwell in the midst of people of unclean lips; for my eyes have seen the King, the Lord of hosts!" [6]Then flew one of the seraphim to me, having in his hand a burning coal which he had taken with tongs from the altar. [7]And he touched my mouth, and said: "Behold, this has touched your lips; your guilt is taken away, and your sin forgiven." [8]And I heard the voice of the Lord saying, "Whom shall I send, and who will go for us?" Then I said, "Here am I! Send me."

Isaiah saw the Lord sitting upon his throne as king (v.1a). This was nothing new in itself, since the holy of holies in a deity's sanctuary was always understood to be an earthly reflection of its heavenly throne, and the deity ruling in heaven was always called by the name of "king."[3] The novelty here lay in God's "aggressiveness":[4] this time he decided to personally take over, bypassing the mediacy of his earthly monarch.

Isaiah saw God overstepping the long-established boundaries, boundaries that he himself had instituted: the train of his kingly robe was not confined to the *debir* (the "holy of holies" or inner sanctuary) where it belonged, but overflowed into the *hekal* (the

---

[3] See Ps 10:16; 24:8-10; 29:10; 44:4; 68:24; 74:12; 84:3; 93:1; 95:3; 98:6; 145:1.
[4] See *OTI₂* 4-6.

"holy" or outer sanctuary; v.1b). Hence he was invading an area reserved for his human servants, the priests of the royal sanctuary. His divine retinue included the *seraphim*,[5] who announced him as the "holy one" par excellence. Paradoxically, this "Holy One," whose holiness consisted in his being totally outside the human realm and unapproachable by humans, was appearing personally to Isaiah. And not just to Isaiah, for his "glory"—another way to say his "presence"[6]—extended throughout the entire earth (v.3), that is to say, throughout the Kingdom of Judah.

Small wonder, then, that Isaiah felt as though he as well as all Judahites were doomed (v.5), for God's holiness could never be compatible with their sinfulness. The hearer should notice that Isaiah considered himself no different from his countrymen in this regard. Also of interest is his reference to "uncleanness of lips." This is clearly in anticipation of the role of Isaiah's lips in the following verses. Indeed, the Lord was not interested in Isaiah himself, but rather in his lips as the instrument to relay God's words verbatim. Isaiah's enthusiastic eagerness to accept the commission offered him (when compared with Jeremiah's reluctance, for instance) need not impress us, as though it might reveal something about Isaiah's character. It is rather to be understood as having been forced upon him by God's anticipation that circumvented any reluctance on Isaiah's part. What the Lord did was to make Isaiah "holy," that is, a member of the "divine council," one of God's "holy ones."[7] We are not told why he did so. A search through the text for some

---

[5] Literally, "the burning ones" (v.2). Their specific role in the "call" of Isaiah will become clear in vv.6-7.

[6] See 1 Kg 8:10-13//2 Chr 5:13-6:2. Notice also the connection there between "glory" and "cloud," which parallels that between "glory" and "smoke" in Is 6:3-4.

[7] See *OTI₂* 45 on the "divine council."

suggestion of special worthiness or preparation on Isaiah's part will prove fruitless. We have here simply an unexplained decision of God—no different from his choosing Jeremiah before that prophet was even born (Jer 1:5). Isaiah realized that his induction into the divine council as a kind of "extraordinary" member had to be for a specific purpose.[8] When the Lord asked the question of v.8a, it became clear that this was the purpose, and Isaiah had no choice but to accept the charge laid upon him (v.8b).

Then came the dreadful message: "Hear and hear, but do not understand; see and see, but do not perceive." (v.9b) God did not want either the Judahites or the Israelites to change their attitude (v.10b), and Isaiah's mission was to make sure of that (v.10a). Why? "Israel does not know, my people does not understand" (1:3b). Isaiah's duty was paradoxically to make the people understand that they *lacked understanding*. His mission was, as it were, to take a snapshot of their situation and then show it to them. The purpose was not to convince them to change their ways; *it was only to show them the justice of the Lord's decision to punish them!*[9] Isaiah was to persevere in his mission of prophecy until God was through with his mission of punishment. It would not be over until the sinful kingdom was destroyed, leaving behind nothing more than a few witnesses to its annihilation (vv.11-13ab):[10]

---

[8] The alternative hardly makes sense: that the Lord would have decided to invite Isaiah to be just a spectator at a session of the divine council, and while there Isaiah would have been moved to volunteer his services before any of the regular members had a chance to say anything!

[9] This is also the purpose of 5:1-7.

[10] See my comments on the "remnant" as witness for total destruction in *OTI₂* 47 and 54.

And though a tenth remain in it, it will be burned again, like a terebinth or an oak, whose stump remains standing when it is felled. The holy seed is its stump. (v.13) *these words are not included in the OSB?*

Since v.13c (The holy seed is its stump) represents a flagrant contradiction to the entire thrust of chapter 6, it is reasonable to construe that it is a comment pointing to those chapters (40-66) dealing with the new Zion.

This initial impression is confirmed by the fact that the word *zera'* (seed, offspring) in the sense of the people of God (as in "offspring of Abraham") occurs only here and at 1:4 in chapters 1-39, but many times in the second part of Isaiah.[11] Although this addition looks ahead to the latter part of the book, it also plays a role within the confines of chapters 1-12:

1. The "holy *zera'* " stands in contradistinction to the "*zera'* of evildoers" condemned in 1:4 who are sentenced to destruction in 6:9-10.

2. The "holiness" of this new seed must be related to the notion of holiness mentioned earlier in chapter 6 and associated with Isaiah himself in vv.6-7. In chapter 8 we learn that Isaiah had some disciples (v.16), that they were called his "children whom the Lord had given" him (v.18a), and that both he and they were "signs and portents in Israel from the Lord" (v.18b). Thus, "holy seed" may refer to the few who accepted the message of God through Isaiah.

---

[11] It is also sometimes translated "descendants" or "children." See Is 41:8; 43:5; 44:3; 45:19, 25; 48:19; 54:3; 59:21; 61:9; 65:9, 23; and especially 66:22. This last instance comes at the conclusion to the Book of Isaiah and is apparently intended to correspond directly to 1:4 in the book's introduction.

3. Chapters 1-12 end with a series of passages whose tone is set by a messianic oracle (11:1-9)[12] that speaks of the eschatological Messiah as "a shoot coming forth from the stump of Jesse" and "a branch growing out of his root" (v.1). The clause in 6:13c must then have had in mind this text that speaks of a new ruler who will revitalize the rotten Davidic dynasty. This finds corroboration in that the earlier reference to a "holy" remnant occurs in conjunction with the new Zion: "And he who is left in Zion and remains in Jerusalem will be called holy, every one who has been recorded for life in Jerusalem." (4:3)

The Sign of še'ar-yašub [A remnant shall return]

7:1In the days of Ahaz the son of Jotham, son of Uzziah, king of Judah, Rezin the king of Syria and Pekah the son of Remaliah the king of Israel came up to Jerusalem to wage war against it, but they could not conquer it. 2When the house of David was told, "Syria is in league with Ephraim," his heart and the heart of his people shook as the trees of the forest shake before the wind. 3And the Lord said to Isaiah, "Go forth to meet Ahaz, you and Shear-jashub your son, at the end of the conduit of the upper pool on the highway to the Fuller's Field, 4and say to him, 'Take heed, be quiet, do not fear, and do not let your heart be faint because of these two smoldering stumps of firebrands, at the fierce anger of Rezin and Syria and the son of Remaliah. 5Because Syria, with Ephraim and the son of Remaliah, has devised evil against you,

---

[12] Notice how each of the following oracles begins with the expression "in that day" (11:10, 11; 12:1), the reference clearly being to the day on which the prophecy of 11:1-9 is fulfilled. The oracle in 11:10 links the word "ensign" to "root of Jesse" in 11:1, the word "ensign" appears again in 11:12, and both are directly related to the survival of the "remnant" in 11:11ff. "Remnant" is a central theme throughout chs.1-12.

saying, [6]"Let us go up against Judah and terrify it, and let us conquer it for ourselves, and set up the son of Tabe-el as king in the midst of it," [7]thus says the Lord God: It shall not stand and it shall not come to pass.

Isaiah's message is relayed through the symbolic names of his children.[13] Isaiah's first child bore the name *še'ar-yašub*, which means "(only) a remnant will return." To what does this refer? Who will return to where? Let us keep in mind that the background of the oracles in chapters 7-8 is the Syro-Ephraimite war against Judah. Given the time frame of that conflict (ca. 735 B.C.), it is hardly possible that these oracles refer to the return of Jerusalemites from the Babylonian exile, which didn't even begin until 587 B.C. Since Isaiah's purpose is to convince King Ahaz that the Lord would preserve Jerusalem from the immediate threat of Syro-Ephraimite aggression, it is unlikely that a divine promise that presupposed the destruction of Jerusalem 150 years later would assuage King Ahaz's fears. On the other hand, to assume that the name *še'ar-yašub* held out the promise of a return to Jerusalem in Ahaz' time, or shortly thereafter, would mean that Isaiah was actually envisaging the destruction of the Judahite capital at the hands of the hostile Syro-Ephraimite alliance. But this plainly contradicts the whole drift of his words in chapter 7, which is to assure Ahaz that no harm will befall Jerusalem. Thus, the only plausible meaning of *še'ar-yašub* is to assume that it refers to the remnant of the Syro-Ephraimite armies that will return to their countries after failing in their attack on Jerusalem. The remnant is not a positive sign of salvation but a negative sign that what was once whole has now been reduced to useless pieces: "As the shepherd rescues from the mouth of the lion two legs, or a piece of an ear, so shall the people of Israel who dwell

---

[13] This is also the case with Hosea (1:3-9).

in Samaria be rescued, with the corner of a couch and part of a bed." (Am 3:12) It is only when the remnant of survivors (Is 1:9) is restored to a new life (4:3) that one can speak of salvation, as in the case of the stump transformed into a seed (6:13).

However, before proceeding to the second sign, the author uses the opportunity of the king's mistrust in the Lord's words of consolation to challenge the following generations of hearers not to follow Ahaz's path. Thus he concludes the passage concerning the sign of *še'ar-yašub* with these words: "If you (plural) will not believe (*ta'aminu*, from the verb *'aman*; trust), surely you (plural) shall not be established (*te'amenu*,[14] from the verb *'aman*; lie in safety, find security)." (v.9b)[15] This concise statement corroborates beyond any doubt what we found earlier regarding the Semitic root *'aman*, namely, that it does not connote mental belief *in* something or someone, but rather trust in (giving credence to) someone's word(s). In the case of the first sign, the Lord's word entailed a promise of safety and security. By switching from the singular to the plural (v.9b), the Lord, through the author, is offering his word of promise to *all* who, in the future, would be willing to accept it.[16] It is important to note here that the Hebrew noun *'emet*, which is usually translated as "truth," is from the same root *'aman*; therefore, God's promise is *truthful* and the safety it will secure is *true* safety as well.

In the absence of any reaction on Ahaz' part (7:3-9a), the conditional offer (v.9b) seems to be a chiding for his lack of

---

[14] This is the same verbal form *niph'al* that is behind *ne'emanah* (faithful, trustworthy; Is 1:21, 26).

[15] The closest to the original Hebrew *'im lo' ta'aminu lo' te'amenu* in preserving the wordplay is the Arabic *'in la tu'amminu lan ta'manu*.

[16] The same device will be used again in dealing with the second sign (vv.10-17). Mark will follow suit in his Gospel: "And what I say to *you* (Peter and James and John and Andrew [who] asked him privately; 13:3) I say to *all*: Watch." (v.37)

commitment and thus lack of trust in the Lord's words. This is validated in the king's reaction to the offer in v.11: "Ask a sign of the Lord your God." This time around Ahaz does not ask for any sign: "I will not ask, and I will not put the Lord to the test." (v.12) This is clearly a facetious remark since God had already given him a sign and he is offering him "again" (v.10) the chance to commit himself. Ahaz' rejection of the sign of *še'ar-yašub* prompted the Lord to provide yet another sign, this time to upbraid the king for his lack of trust rather than to reassure him.

The Messianic Sign of Immanuel   First Sign

The reference to "Immanuel" in Isaiah 7:10-17 is among the most famous texts in the Old Testament, but scholars have yet to reach a consensus on its meaning.[17] Nevertheless, I believe a solution to understanding this puzzling text is possible when one gives serious consideration to the obvious deliberate parallelism between chapters 7 and 8. Consider the following:

1. Chapters 7 and 8 each contain two oracles linked together in the same way: "And the Lord said to..." (7:3//8:1)[18] introduces the first, while "Again the Lord spoke to..." (7:10//8:5)[19] begins the second.

---

[17] The exceptional complexity of this passage is mirrored in the wide variety of interpretations given to it, as compared to the virtually unanimous agreement among interpreters in their understanding of the other three oracles in chs.7-8.

[18] RSV has "then" in 8:1 rather than "and" but the Hebrew word it translates is the same in both instances.

[19] The word order is different in the RSV translation but identical in Hebrew. The only difference is an additional word, *'od* (again) in 8:5. This is due to the fact that the addressee in ch.8 is Isaiah in both instances, whereas in ch.7 the addressees are Isaiah in 7:3 and Ahaz in 7:10. The extra adverb is not reflected in the English translation because it would be redundant: "Again the Lord spoke to me again ..."

2. The first sign in each chapter is a child of Isaiah's
   (7:3; 8:1, 3), and both signs apply to the
   kingdoms of Israel and Aram.

3. In both chapters, the second sign (7:10-17) or
   oracle (8:5-8) concerns Judah. Moreover, each
   entails, either indirectly (ch.7) or directly (ch.8),
   a divine judgment against the lack of faith
   exhibited toward the first sign. In other words, in
   each chapter the second oracle is triggered by the
   rejection of the first.

Originally, the second sign offered by Isaiah was the following:
a (Jerusalemite) woman who happens to be pregnant[20] will name
her son 'immanu'el (God is with us) in recognition of the divine
intervention Ahaz did not believe would happen—by the time
the child reaches the age of "knowledge of good and evil" (vv.14,
16)[21] the Syro-Ephraimite threat will have been neutralized.
Alternatively, however, v.14 could be a general reference to
"women who are now pregnant," but the meaning would be the
same. Such an interpretation takes into consideration the fact
that in Hebrew the definite article followed by a singular noun is
often generic, i.e., it refers to everything fitting the category
described by the noun. Thus, e.g., hakkena'ani (the Canaanite)
means "the Canaanites."[22] Consequently, ha'olmah in v.14 may
well be generic in the same way ("women" rather than "the

---

[20] Both harah (pregnant) and yoledet (giving birth) are participles and are linked by the
conjunction we (and), which indicates a proximate delivery.

[21] This is simply a way of specifying a certain stage in one's life, most probably "the age of
weaning." Weaning in the Ancient Near East took place much later than it does nowadays
in the Western civilizations (see 1 Sam 1:22-24); according to 2 Macc 7:27, it was done at
the age of three.

[22] See Gen 10:19; 12:6; 13:7; etc. While English translations have the plural "Canaanites"
or "Perizzites," the Hebrew has "the Canaanite" or "the Perizzite."

woman"). Moreover, had the child intended by Isaiah been either his own or Ahaz', one would have expected the text to be more straightforward—especially since the immediate context (chs.7-8) explicitly mentions both Isaiah's wife and sons, on the one hand (7:3; 8:1, 3), and Ahaz as the addressee of the oracle, on the other.

Ahaz did not heed the second sign either, and his obstinacy gave a renewed chance for the author to address the same divine offer to the following generations of the royal "house of David" (7:13a). Such is noticeable in the back and forth switch between the second person singular and the second person plural:

> [10]Again the Lord spoke to Ahaz, [11]"Ask (singular) a sign of the Lord your (singular) God; let it be deep as Sheol or high as heaven." [12]But Ahaz said, "I will not ask, and I will not put the Lord to the test." [13]And he said, "Hear (plural) then, O house of David! Is it too little for you (plural) to weary men, that you weary (plural) my God also? [14]Therefore the Lord himself will give you (plural) a sign. Behold, a young woman shall conceive and bear a son, and shall call his name Immanuel. [15]He shall eat curds and honey when he knows how to refuse the evil and choose the good. [16]For before the child knows how to refuse the evil and choose the good, the land before whose two kings you are (singular) in dread will be deserted. [17]The Lord will bring upon you (singular) and upon your (singular) people and upon your (singular) father's house such days as have not come since the day that Ephraim departed from Judah—the king of Assyria."

Thus, beyond the punishment of Ahaz and the kingdom during his reign (v.17) due to the king's lack of trust in the Lord's first sign (v.16b), the sign of Immanuel will nevertheless hold hope for future generations (vv.13-14) should they trust in it. Still, because Ahaz did not heed the second sign, his attitude occasioned a third sign borne by another child of Isaiah's (8:1-8), which sign has been prepared for in the mention of the king of Assyria at the end of 7:17. Assyria, from which Ahaz thought to get help against the Syro-Ephraimite coalition, will later invade Judah with devastating results.

The Sign of maher-šalal-ḥaš-baz [*The spoil speeds, the prey hastes*]

8:1Then the Lord said to me, "Take a large tablet and write upon it in common characters, 'Belonging to Maher-shal'al-hash-baz'" 2And I got reliable witnesses, Uriah the priest and Zechariah the son of Jeberechiah, to attest for me. 3And I went to the prophetess, and she conceived and bore a son. Then the Lord said to me, "Call his name Maher-shal'al-hash-baz: 4for before the child knows how to cry 'My father' or 'My mother,' the wealth of Damascus and the spoil of Samaria will be carried away before the king of Assyria."

Even after Isaiah offered him two "signs" reassuring him of the Lord's commitment to protect his city, Ahaz remained distrustful. What was called for after this was no longer reassurance, but rather condemnation of the king for his disbelief. But how could Isaiah chastise the king without proving him wrong? And how could Ahaz be proven wrong until the Syro-Ephraimite threat melted away without harming Jerusalem? That was still in the future, so a new sign simply condemning the king for his distrust would have been unconvincing at best and unjust at worst. The time would come when everyone would be able to see if the Lord honored his promise—but what could be done before then? All Isaiah could do, and what he did do, was to repeat the message already offered twice before. The function of the *maher-šalal-ḥaš-baz* sign in 8:1-4 is identical to that of the *še'ar-yašub* sign: it proclaims that the Syro-Ephraimite alliance is no threat at all to Jerusalem. The two oracles are

Shear jashub - a remnant shall return
maher shalal hashbaz - quickly despoil, swiftly plunder

different, though, in that the second one emphasizes God's control of the situation:

1. Whereas Ahaz is the main addressee of both signs in chapter 7, he is curiously absent from the entire picture in chapter 8.

2. Unlike the first child of Isaiah, his second is conceived at the express request of the Lord (8:1). That is to say, the Lord himself is the initiator of the sign and therefore of the event it signifies as well—the Assyrian conquest of Aram *(Syria)* and Israel (v.4; see also v.7).

3. The second oracle (vv.5-8) follows immediately as if it were a continuation of the first, which in fact it is since (a) both speak of the same invasion by Assyria, and (b) the lack of faith denounced in v.6 is not something new but rather the same as the original unbelieving response of Ahaz to the sign of *še'ar-yašub*. In this second oracle, the emphasis is on the Lord's direct action: "the Lord is bringing up against them ... the king of Assyria." (v.7)

There is one other difference between the two signs of *še'ar-yašub* and *maher-šalal-ḥaš-baz:* unlike the former, which applied strictly to Aram and Israel, the latter includes Judah in its purview. The king of Assyria who was going to invade Judah's enemies, Israel and Syria, would also "sweep on into Judah" itself (v.8a).[23]

---

[23] Note that no fourth sign precedes the fourth oracle: both the third and fourth oracles interpret the third sign. See also in 8:14 the reference to "both houses of Israel."

The official nature of the sign of *maher-šalal-ḥaš-baz* is underscored in that it is consigned to a document written on a "large tablet" for all to see (v.1) and is sealed in the presence of two witnesses (v.2). Moreover the witnesses are "reliable" (*ne'emanim*; trustworthy) and thus reflective of the "faithful (*ne'emanah*; trustworthy) city," Zion (1:21, 26).[24] Furthermore, their names are functional. Besides being a priest, representative of the temple where the Lord who dislodged Uzziah appeared to Isaiah (6:1), the name of the first witness, Uriah (*'uriyyah*), means "the Lord is my light" and thus represents those of "the house of Jacob" who walk in "the light of the Lord" (*'or yahweh*; 2:5) by following his law and teaching (v.3). The second witness is Zechariah (*zekaryahu*; the Lord remembered), the son of Jeberechiah (*yeberekyahu*; the Lord shall bless); that is to say, whenever the Lord remembers the promise he issued through Isaiah, he will bring about the blessing of salvation. In turn, the last name *yeberekyahu* seals the link between the two signs of *še'ar-yašub* and *maher-šalal-ḥaš-baz* since in 8:1 and 7:3 we hear of the only two instances in chapters 1-12 of the Hebrew root *brk*: "Go forth to meet Ahaz, you and Shear-jashub your son, at the end of the conduit of the upper pool (*berekah*)[25] on the highway to the Fuller's Field."

From these observations it becomes clear that Isaiah's main message is in chapter 8, to which chapter 7 serves as a preamble. This conclusion is corroborated by the fact that the expression "this people" which figures prominently in Isaiah's "call" (6:9, 10) occurs only here (8:6, 11, 12). Likewise, the reference to the

---

[24] It is the same adjective: *ne'emanim* is masculine plural and *ne'emanah* feminine singular.

[25] The same four consonants *brkh*, vocalized differently, mean "blessing" (*berakah*) or "pool" (*berekah*).

holiness of the Lord of hosts in 8:13 and to his dwelling on
Mount Zion in 8:18, harks back to Isaiah's vision in 6:1-5. That
is to say, chapter 6 anticipates chapter 8, and Isaiah's mission in
chapter 8 fulfills his commission in chapter 6. In both instances,
due to the bankruptcy of its kingship, the Lord takes the destiny
of Judah into his own hands.

8:5The Lord spoke to me again, 6"Because this people have refused
the waters of Shiloah that flow gently, and melt in fear before
Rezin and the son of Remaliah; therefore, behold, the Lord is
bringing up against them the waters of the River, mighty and
many, the king of Assyria and all his glory; and it will rise over all
its channels and go over all its banks; 8and it will sweep on into
Judah, it will overflow and pass on, reaching even to the neck; and
its outspread wings will fill the breadth of your land, O
Immanuel." 9Be broken, you peoples, and be dismayed; give ear,
all you far countries; gird yourselves and be dismayed; gird
yourselves and be dismayed. 10Take counsel together, but it will
come to nought; speak a word, but it will not stand, for God is
with us. 11For the Lord spoke thus to me with his strong hand
upon me, and warned me not to walk in the way of this people
saying: 12"Do not call conspiracy all that this people call
conspiracy, and to not fear what they fear, nor be in dread. 13But
the Lord of hosts, him you shall regard as holy; let him be your
fear, and let him be your dread. 14And he will become a sanctuary,
and a stone of offense, and a rock of stumbling to both houses of
Israel, a trap and a snare to the inhabitants of Jerusalem. 15And
many shall stumble thereon; they shall fall and be broken; they
shall be snared and taken." 16Bind up the testimony, seal the
teaching among my disciples. 17I will wait for the Lord, who is
hiding his face from the house of Jacob, and I will hope in him.
18Behold, I and the children whom the Lord has given me are
signs and portents in Israel from the Lord of hosts, who dwells on
Mount Zion.

Despite Isaiah's confidence that he was accurately relating what the Lord certainly would do in his own time, there was no way he could prove to anyone else that he was right. In fact he was very much alone in his views (vv.11-15). When he confronted Ahaz, it still seemed obvious to everyone that the Syro-Ephraimite alliance was about to overpower Judah and Jerusalem. If Isaiah's position was to be proven at all, it would only be in the future, by looking at it retrospectively. So for the time being his message had to be consigned to a more permanent medium than the spoken word: it had to become a written "word." This "testimony," entitled *lemaher-šalal-ḥaš-baz* (belonging to/concerning *maher-šalal-ḥaš-baz*), was to be bound up and sealed in the presence of two official witnesses as Isaiah's teaching left to his disciples (v.16; see v.2). This is the first instance where we are expressly told that a prophetic "word" was consigned to writing, that is, as scripture. By doing so Isaiah committed not only himself but also God to that word, for better (if the Lord made good on his promise) or for worse (if future events proved the promise to be an empty one). As it turned out, his trust was not misplaced. In time the Lord fulfilled his promise, and Isaiah's word was vindicated long after his death. In the meantime, all Isaiah could do was keep silent regarding the matter and wait in hope (v.17). He and his disciples would themselves function as the signs through whom the Lord of hosts would remind the people of the message he had sent them at the hand of Isaiah (v.18).

Although the "word of God spoken to Isaiah"[26] would, in fact, be vindicated, does that mean the word once vindicated would not be relevant for any other purpose? No; not at all. God's word was not to be disposed of so lightly. Instead, it was to live on

---

[26] See 8:1, 5, 11. See also 6:8, 9, 11; 7:3, 10, 13.

among Isaiah's disciples, who read and accepted this "scripture" as presenting the "word of God"—not as a historical record of what had *already* been fulfilled in the past, but rather of what was still awaiting fulfillment in the future, even among generations that would not witness either the original confrontation or the original vindication:

> And when they say to you, "Consult the mediums and the wizards who chirp and mutter," should not a people consult their God? Should they consult the dead on behalf of the living? To the teaching and to the testimony! Surely for this word which they speak there is no dawn. (vv.19-20)

And, as usual, the divine word is free to all who would want to make use of it and enjoy its blessings. The alternative is not neutrality, for in scripture there are no "grey areas"—there is light and darkness, life or death. In this case, those who will not accept Isaiah's scripturalized "teaching" (vv.16, 20) will be walking in "darkness" (vv.21-23)

Immanuel

First Sign

The noun "Immanuel" represents arguably the most classic case of philosophical theologizing that in time has affected all strands of Christianity. Let us look at how the translations, starting with the LXX, render the three occurrences of *'immanu-'el* (with us [is] God) in the same context:

LXX

> Therefore the Lord himself will give you a sign. Behold, a young woman shall conceive and bear a son, and shall call his name *Emmanouēl.* (7:14)

> and it will sweep on into Judah, it will overflow and pass on, reaching even to the neck; and its outspread wings will fill the

breadth of your land, *meth' hēmōn ho Theos* (with us [is] God).
(8:8)

Take counsel together, but it will come to nought; speak a word,
but it will not stand, for *meth' hēmōn kyrios ho Theos* (with us [is]
the Lord God). (8:10)

KJV

Therefore the Lord himself shall give you a sign; Behold, a virgin
shall conceive, and bear a son, and shall call his name Immanuel.
(7:14)

And he shall pass through Judah; he shall overflow and go over, he
shall reach *even* to the neck; and the stretching out of his wings
shall fill the breadth of thy land, O Immanuel. (8:8)

Take counsel together, and it shall come to nought; speak the
word, and it shall not stand: for God *is* with us. (8:10)

JB

The Lord will give you a sign in any case: It is this: the young
woman is with child and will give birth to a son whom she will
call Immanuel. (7:14)

it will flow into Judah, flooding everything and passing on; it will
reach right up to the neck, and the spreading of its wings will
cover the whole extent of your country, Immanuel! (8:8)

Devise plans as you may: they will come to nothing! Make what
pronouncements you like; it will not come about! For God is with
us! (8:10)

RSV

Therefore the Lord himself will give you a sign. Behold, a young woman shall conceive and bear a son, and shall call his name Immanuel. (7:14)

and it will sweep on into Judah, it will overflow and pass on, reaching even to the neck; and its outspread wings will fill the breadth of your land, O Immanuel. (8:8)

Take counsel together, but it will come to nought; speak a word, but it will not stand, for God is with us. (8:10)

Systematically, all the above referenced translations have "God is with us" in 8:10, obviously understanding it as a statement. However, all render the first instance (7:14) as "Immanuel." Except for the LXX, a hearer unaware of the original language will deduce that the first two instances (7:14; 8:8) refer to an individual whose name is "Immanuel" or "Emmanuel," whereas in 8:10 the same hearer perceives the exact same original as that statement, "God [is, will be] with us."[27] At least the LXX, which I repeatedly dub in my commentaries as the most intelligent translation of the original Hebrew, piques the hearer's curiosity by rendering the unquestionably vocative[28] *'immanu-'el* in 8:8 unexpectedly as a statement: *meth' hēmōn ho Theos* (with us [is] God). The hearer of the LXX cannot but be "thrown off" and inquire, at least mentally, as to what is going on. At rehearing, a perceptive hearer will eventually realize the "with us [is] God" in "and it will sweep on into *Judah*, it will overflow and pass on, reaching even to the neck; and its outspread wings will fill the breadth of *your land*, O 'with us [is] God'" (8:8) is none other than *Emmanouēl* (Immanuel) of 7:14. However, by the same

---

[27] Even the Van Dyke Arabic translation follows suit.
[28] See "O Immanuel" in both KJV and RSV.

token, that same hearer will also notice the connection with the following *meth' hēmōn kyrios ho Theos* (with us [is] the Lord God; v.10).

Still the original is much more direct especially that in Semitic languages there are no uppercase letters; consequently there are no so-called "proper" names. It is only from the context of a passage that the hearer is able to figure out whether an actual person is intended, or a function, or possibly both, in case of wordplay.[29] The equivalence between a so-called personal name and a noun is more pronounced in Arabic that uses word declensions[30] even when the intended is a personal name; this is also done in Greek and Latin.[31] Given that the young woman about to give birth in 7:14 is generic, and thus unidentified, it stands to reason to consider that her "son," especially with a name like "With us [is] God," is also unidentified. It is a person through whose mediacy God will be with his people, should the people accept God's previous challenge to all at the occasion of the threat posed by Rezin and the son of Remaliah (7:1-9a): "If you (plural) will not believe, surely you (plural) shall not be established." (v.9b).[32] But the people failed: "Because this people

---

[29] Two examples will clarify my point. Let's say a young man just won the soccer state championship and his father greets him with "Oh my victor (victorious one)"; now let us assume that the young man's name is Victor, then the greeting "Oh my Victor" has a double connotation. The same applies in the case of an elderly sick mother who is visited by her caring daughter whom she addresses as "Oh my hope (in life)"; if the daughter's name was Hope, then the connotation is even more forceful: "Oh my Hope!" However, in both cases, even a stranger who does not know the names of the children will still get the same basic message.

[30] In the study of languages "declension" refers to "the inflection of nouns, pronouns, and adjectives in such categories as case, number, and gender."

[31] Thus, the same proper name *muhammad* would have a different ending depending on its function in the phrase or sentence: (a) *muhammadun* ate; (b) I saw *muhammadan*; (c) the book of *muhammadin* (d) I spoke for (or about) *muhammadin*.

[32] See earlier my comments on that verse.

Siloam

have refused the waters of Shiloah that flow gently, and melt in fear before Rezin and the son of Remaliah." (8:6) That is why "the Lord is bringing up against them the waters of the River, mighty and many, the king of Assyria and all his glory" (v.7). That is also why the promise that God would be with his people and his intervention on their behalf against the threatening nations is postponed (vv.9-10). However, when he does intervene, the end result of that intervention will encompass not only the Assyrians, but also many "peoples" and "far countries" who will be brought under the Lord's aegis. Put otherwise, the promise in vv.9-10 is looking beyond the people's refusal to a time subsequent to the scripturalization of Isaiah's teaching (vv.11-20), a time when the light of that teaching will reach into "the Galilee of the nations" (9:1), that is to say, the time when the Law will be shared with all nations as well as with the Judahite exiles (42:1-7; 49:5-6), as was already predicted in 2:2-4. And such will take place under the leadership of the "son" whose name is "With us [is] God."

The Second Messianic Sign

Second Sign Isaiah 9

⁹:⁶For to us a child is born, to us a son is given; and the government will be upon his shoulder, and his name will be called, "Wonderful Counselor, Mighty God, Everlasting Father, Prince of Peace." ⁷Of the increase of his government and of peace there will be no end, upon the throne of David, and over his kingdom, to establish it, and to uphold it with justice and with righteousness from this time forth and for evermore. The zeal of the Lord of hosts will do this.

In speaking of the leader whose "name will be called (*yiqra' šemo*) 'Wonderful Counselor, Mighty God (*'el*), Everlasting Father, Prince of Peace'" we are told "to us (*lanu*) a child (*yeled*) is born (*yullad*), to us (*lanu*) a son (*ben*) is given" (9:6). This vocabulary clearly corresponds to that of 7:14b: "Behold, a young woman shall conceive and bear (*yoledet*) a son (*ben*), and shall call his name (*qara't šemo*) 'With us (*'immanu*) [is] God (*'el*)." That someone who sits "upon the throne of David, and over his kingdom" (9:7) would be referred to as "(Mighty) God" (v.6) should not surprise us, since this is obviously an honorific title; it comes second in a series of four "kingly" titles. This is corroborated in Psalm 45:6a: "Thy throne, O God, *is* for ever and ever (KJV as well as LXX)."[33] So God will be "with" (for) his people at a later time when he will gather all nations together with his "people, the house of Jacob" (Is 2:6). All along it is God himself who is the agent of the entire plan. The chosen "son of David" is just the medium through whom God implements his will, as is evident in the ending of 9:6: "The zeal of the Lord of hosts will do this."

Samaria and the Northern Kingdom

Between the second "messianic" sign (vv.6-7) and the third "messianic" prophecy (11:1-9) concerning a forthcoming "son of David," Isaiah has a lengthy passage about the punishment of Samaria and its eventual restoration along with the indictment of its punishing agent, Assyria (9:8-10:34). At one point in the description of the destruction, together with a promise of deliverance, we hear no less than five references in a row to *še'ar* (remnant), two of which are *še'ar yašub* (a remnant will return):

> [10:18]The glory of his forest and of his fruitful land the Lord will destroy, both soul and body, and it will be as when a sick man wastes away. [19]The remnant (*še'ar*) of the trees of his forest will be so few that a child can write them down. [20]In that day the remnant (*še'ar*) of Israel and the survivors of the house of Jacob

---

[33] RSV softens the blow by translating: "Your divine throne endures for ever and ever."

will no more lean upon him that smote them, but will lean upon the Lord, the Holy One of Israel, in truth. [21]A remnant will return (*še'ar yašub*), the remnant (*še'ar*) of Jacob, to the mighty God. [22]For though your people Israel be as the sand of the sea, only a remnant of them will return (*še'ar yašub*). Destruction is decreed, overflowing with righteousness. [23]For the Lord, the Lord of hosts, will make a full end, as decreed, in the midst of all the earth. [24]Therefore thus says the Lord, the Lord of hosts: "O my people, who dwell in Zion, be not afraid of the Assyrians when they smite with the rod and lift up their staff against you as the Egyptians did. [25]For in a very little while my indignation will come to an end, and my anger will be directed to their destruction."

It is obvious even in the English translation that the previous negative *še'ar yašub*, describing the unsuccessful incursion of the forces of Samaria into Judah (7:2-9), is turned into a positive *še'ar yašub* to describe the remnant that will become part of the new Zion (10:24) after the city's subsequent fall to Assyria. This rejoins what we found in 4:2-6. However, in this case one senses not only a concern about Samaria, but also a push to include the other "nations." This can be detected in the phraseology of the introductory verse to the passage describing the restoration of the northern kingdom: "But there will be no gloom for her that was in anguish. In the former time he brought into contempt the land of Zebulun and the land of Naphtali, but in the latter time he will make glorious the way of the sea, the land beyond (*'eber*; across) the Jordan, Galilee of the nations (*gelil* [circle, district] *haggoyim*)." (9:1) According to the allotment of the tribes in Joshua, the inheritances of Zebulon (19:10-16) and Naphtali (vv.32-39) fell in the northernmost part of Canaan and, by the same token, the northernmost parts of the Kingdom of Israel, away from its capital Samaria. The author's intent in mentioning these tribes is to stress that God would not forget even the most forgettable people. Still, a closer look at the map of allotment will show that the phraseology of Isaiah 9:1 reflects a "movement" away from the central part of Canaan toward the Jordan river and "beyond (across)" it toward Trans-Jordan. In the original Hebrew the *gelil haggoyim* (literally meaning the "area where the nations reside"), more specifically Assyria, Babylon, and Medo-Persia, are clearly in Isaiah's purview. This mission to carry God's law to the nations will fall upon the servant of the Lord in Second-Isaiah (42:1-7; 49:6). This is confirmed in 9:1, a few verses after we are told about the "law" (*torah*) that Isaiah consigned into a scroll with the hope that future generations would hearken to its contents (8:16-20).

The Messianic Prophecy of Universal Peace

The third and final "messianic" prophecy (ch.11) recapitulates the message of the previous chapters and prepares for the second part of the book (chs.40-66), beyond the disobedience of Hezekiah who followed in his father Ahaz' footsteps by showing lack of trust in God's promise (chs.36-39). The promised eschatological leader is usually portrayed as either David or the son of David. Here in Isaiah 11, we have the only reference to that leader as being a descendant of Jesse, David's father (1 Sam 16:19-20). The intentionality of such is evident in that (1) Jesse is referred to twice (vv.1, 10) for underscoring, (2) these are the only occurrences of that name in the Latter Prophets, and (3) the total absence of David in that chapter. The aim is to present the "Prince of (universal) Peace" (9:6) as *another* David, a "new" David, on a par with David himself, that is, someone *directly* brought about by God, rather than someone indirectly established through the Davidic succession.[34] It is as though God will be turning the page and starting a new chapter, a new era.

---

[34] See Ezek 34:23-24; 37:24-25 and my comments thereon in *C-Ezek*.

This new leader will be filled sevenfold with the spirit of the Lord (11:2), and especially with the spirit of the "fear of the Lord"—that is to say, obedient to his law[35]—which is underscored through repetition (vv.2-3). Furthermore his reign of justice will be indeed universal since it will extend even over the animal realm (vv.6-8) that shares *equally* God's created realm with the human beings (Gen 1:24-31). Put otherwise, the hoped for universal peace around the Lord's holy mountain (Is 2:2-4) will finally be realized (11:9) when the "knowledge of the Lord" in his law and teaching (2:3b) will fill the earth (11:9b).

The further description of the result of that reign is cast in terminology reminiscent of that used in the previous chapters regarding the "remnant" (vv.11 and 16), the equal status between Ephraim (Israel) and Judah (v.13), and the inclusion of all nations:[36]

> [10]In that day the root of Jesse shall stand as an ensign to the peoples; him shall the nations seek, and his dwellings shall be glorious. [11]In that day the Lord will extend his hand yet a second time to recover the remnant (*še'ar*) which is left (*yiśśa'er*) of his people, from Assyria, from Egypt, from Pathros, from Ethiopia, from Elam, from Shinar, from Hamath, and from the coastlands of the sea. [12]He will raise an ensign for the nations, and will assemble the outcasts of Israel, and gather the dispersed of Judah from the four corners of the earth. [13]The jealousy of Ephraim shall depart, and those who harass Judah shall be cut off; Ephraim shall not be jealous of Judah, and Judah shall not harass Ephraim. [14]But they shall swoop down upon the shoulder of the Philistines in the west, and together they shall plunder the people of the east. They shall put forth their hand against Edom and Moab, and the Ammonites shall obey them. [15]And the Lord will utterly destroy

---

[35] See *OTI₃* 130.
[36] Notice the thrice reference to "peoples" (v.10) and nations" (vv.10, 12).

the tongue of the sea of Egypt; and will wave his hand over the River with his scorching wind, and smite it into seven channels that men may cross dryshod. ¹⁶And there will be a highway from Assyria for the remnant (še'ar) which is left (yišša'er) of his people, as there was for Israel when they came up from the land of Egypt.

Moreover, as mentioned earlier in my discussion of chapters 9 and 10, it is more specifically Samaria and the kingdom of Israel that are in the purview of the restoration. Such is evident in that the repeated reference to the "remnant (še'ar) which is left (yišša'er) of his people" is made in conjunction with "from Assyria" (11:11 and 16). A further indication can be found in that the earlier "signal" (nes) for a "nation far off" (5:26), which is Assyria, to punish Samaria is now turned into an "ensign" (nes) to the peoples (11:10) and for the nations (v.12) to assemble around his dwellings (v.11) in peace (2:2-4).[37]

Psalm of Praise

¹²:¹You [singular] will[38] say in that day: "I will give thanks to thee, O Lord, for though thou wast angry with me, thy anger turned away, and thou didst comfort me. ²Behold, God is my salvation; I will trust, and will not be afraid; for the Lord God is my strength and my song, and he has become my salvation." ³With joy you [plural] will draw water from the wells of salvation. ⁴And you [plural] will say in that day: 'Give [plural] thanks to the Lord, call upon his name; make known his deeds among the nations, proclaim that his name is exalted. ⁵Sing praises to the Lord, for he has done gloriously; let this be known in all the earth. ⁶Shout and sing for joy, O inhabitant of Zion, for great in your midst is the Holy One of Israel."

---

[37] These are the only instances of nes in chs.1-12.
[38] RSV has simply "You will," whereas KJV reads "thou shalt say" and JB translates "tu diras."

The hope for such universal peace around the divine mountain warrants a concluding psalm of praise to the Lord, which looks ahead to the divine consolation starting with chapter 40, harks back to the first chapter of the book, and is replete with the central vocabulary that controlled the odyssey of chapters 1-11. It would be worth our while to analyze every verse to get the feel of how this short passage would have sounded to the hearers of the original. Let me begin by pointing out that the passage is divided in two parts each introduced with "you will say in that day," with the difference being that the first call is individualized (v.1a), whereas the second is addressed to the congregation (v.4a). So the call to acknowledge God's salvation is issued to each individual, yet the enjoyment of that salvation is collective (v.3); in turn this collective joy will be expressed in a communal thanksgiving uttered by the many children of the one city, the new Zion[39] (v.6). In English this last verse sounds as though it is addressed to an individual, however, understanding it as such does not fit with the following "in your midst," which is usually used of a community or a city. When one considers that "inhabitant" in Hebrew is the grammatically feminine *yošebet*, then one realizes that "inhabitant (fem) of Zion" is tantamount to "daughter of Zion" (1:8; 10:32), a metaphoric representation of the city, which is the grammatically feminine noun *'ir* in Hebrew. Thus in 12:1-2 each individual is called upon as a son or a daughter of the new Zion (49:22), which encompasses nations as well as Judahites and Israelites, as we have seen in 11:10-16. That is why the first duty of the collective, after calling upon the Lord's name (12:4a), is to "make known his deeds among the nations (*'ammim*; peoples)" and "proclaim that

---

[39] Is 49:13-26; 54:1-10.

his name is exalted" (v.4b) Looking at the vocabulary in more detail, we find the following:

1. In v.1 "anger" (*'aph*) harks back to the twice mentioned "anger" in 5:25, while "comfort" (*tenaḥameni*) presages the opening verse of the second part of the book: "Comfort, comfort (*naḥamu naḥamu*) my people, says your God." (40:1)

2. In turn God's consolation expressed through "salvation" mentioned thrice, thus controlling as well as bracketing 12:2-3, is a staple of chapters 40-66.

3. V.2 is much richer than first strikes the ear. The Hebrew *yešu'ah* (salvation) is from the same root as *yeša'yahu* (Isaiah; the Lord will save). So the Lord's salvation will come about through Isaiah's teaching that was refused by the king (ch.7) and the people (8:11-12), yet was consigned to scripture for the following generations (vv.16-22). Only to the extent that each person trusts (*baṭaḥ*; 12:2)[40] in that teaching will he no longer "be afraid" (*paḥad*) "before the terror (*paḥad*) of the Lord" (2:10, 19, 21). The reason is that "my strength" (*'ozzi*) will be "the Lord" (*yahweh*; *yah* for short)[41] and not King Uzziah (*'uzzi-yahu*; the Lord is my strength). My readers are reminded

---

[40] *baṭaḥ* has the same connotation of trust as the verb *'aman* used in 7:9a; see my comments earlier.

[41] Both forms occur in Hebrew 12:2.

that it is the Lord who appeared to Isaiah as *the King*, not King Uzziah (6:1).[42]

4. Joy as related to water (12:3) occurs several times in Second-Isaiah; themes of joy and abundance of water abound throughout that part of the book (48:20-21; 49:10-13; 55:1-12).

5. Finally, the Holy One of Israel, who was despised (1:4; 5:24) and mocked by the people (5:19), will abide in the midst of them in the new Zion (12:6) when "in that day" (vv.1, 4) "its inhabitant" (v.6) will have repented and learned to truly rely on him: "In that day the remnant of Israel and the survivors of the house of Jacob will no more lean upon him that smote them, but will lean upon the Lord, the Holy One of Israel, in truth." (10:20)[43]

---

[42] See my earlier comments on that verse.

[43] These five instances account for the all the occurrences of "The Holy one of Israel" in Is 1-12.

Chapter 4

Oracles concerning the Nations

Isaiah 13

In the Latter Prophets, the function of the oracles about the nations is to underscore the Lord's universal hegemony over all peoples and their deities (Ps 82).[1] The heading in Isaiah 13:1, "The oracle concerning Babylon which Isaiah the son of Amoz saw," intentionally mimics that of chapter 2:1 (The word which Isaiah the son of Amoz saw). This is done to impress upon the hearer that chapters 13-23 have the same teaching value as chapters 2-12.[2] The link between these two sections is further secured through the qualification of the first oracle as a "signal" (*nes*; 13:2), which is the same word that just occurred twice to speak of the message of peace that would include the nations (ensign [*nes*]; 11:10, 12). *(p. 98)*

Babylon

Leading the list is the oracle addressed to Babylon (Is 13-14; 21:1-10), the powerful nation that eventually would destroy Jerusalem (39:5-7). The oracle is basically cast in the same phraseology as the one used against Judah and Jerusalem: the day of the Lord (13:6, 9), darkness (v.10), the humiliation of "the haughtiness (*ga'awah*) of the ruthless" (v.11), and the likening of Babylon to Sodom and Gomorrah (v.19). The only additional feature is the universal, if not, cosmic aspects of the divine army (vv.4-5), which sounds similar to that raised against Gog of Magog in Ezekiel (38:18-23). This universality is further

---

[1] See *OTI₂* 32-35; *C-Ezek* 283-90, 311-26.

[2] This is precisely where classical "theology" errs: it reads scripture as proof texts to support its view concerning certain topics, rather than simply "hearing" scripture "out."

underscored by the use of "Almighty" (*šadday*; Is 13:6) to speak of God, which is its only occurrence in the book.[3]

Before dealing more specifically with the demise of the King of Babylon (Is 14:3-23), the author sidetracks to speak of the outcome of the destruction of Babylon: the end of Jacob's exile. This short passage (vv.1-2) covers, in a nutshell, the message of the second part of Isaiah:

> [1]The Lord will have compassion (*yeraḥḥem*) on Jacob and will again choose (*baḥar*) Israel, and will set them in their own land, and aliens will join (*nilwah*) them and will cleave to the house of Jacob. [2]And the peoples will take them and bring them to their place, and the house of Israel will possess them in the Lord's land as male and female slaves; they will take captive those who were their captors, and rule over those who oppressed them.

The opening verse (1a) uses two Hebrew verbs, *riḥḥem* (have mercy on) and *baḥar* (choose), that are staples of Second-Isaiah. In the same verse we hear what is stressed throughout the prophetic books time and again, namely, that the nations will join Israel in the new Zion: "aliens will join (*nilwah*; from the verb *lawah*) them and will cleave to the house of Jacob" (v.1b). The other two instances of the verb *lawah* occur in 56:3 and 6-7:

> Let not the foreigner who has joined himself (*nilwah*) to the Lord say, "The Lord will surely separate me from his people"; and let not the eunuch say, "Behold, I am a dry tree" ... And the foreigners who join themselves (*nilwah*) to the Lord, to minister to him, to love the name of the Lord, and to be his servants, every one who keeps the sabbath, and does not profane it, and holds fast my covenant—these I will bring to my holy mountain, and make them joyful in my house of prayer; their burnt offerings and their

---

[3] *šadday* is a staple of Job, the book of God's universality par excellence.

sacrifices will be accepted on my altar; for my house shall be called a house of prayer for all peoples.

The same thought is revisited in 66:21 where we hear that the Lord "will take some of them [your brethren from among the nations] for priests and for Levites (*lewiyyim*; from the same root as *lawah*)."[4] This being the case, it is unfortunate that RSV translates 14:2 in a way that gives the impression that the nations would be subjugated by Israel. Such would blatantly contradict v.1b.

I shall try to render the meaning of v.2 from the original Hebrew, beginning with a literal translation: "And peoples will take them and bring them into their place, and the house of Israel will inherit them (*hitnahalum*) as servants and handmaids on the Lord's ground (*'adamah*); they will bring as captives (in exile; *sobim* from the verb *šabah*) those who took them into exile (*šobehem*), and rule (*radu*) over those who oppressed them (*nogšehem*)." In view of the integration of the nations with the house of Israel on the Lord's ground, we are told, "peoples will take them and bring them into their place," obviously under the command of Cyrus, God's appointee (41:1-5; 44:24-45:7). In turn, those peoples and nations will become an integral part of the inheritance (*nahalah*) allocated to Israel, where those nations will be serving the Lord's house (Is 66:21). Notice how Israel's "ground" (*'adamah*; [land in RSV] Is 14:1) is an inheritance, and not a possession, since v.2 makes it clear that that "ground" (*'adamah*) is the Lord's; he is the sole King (*melek*; proprietor), which is a point stressed repeatedly in Isaiah (6:5; 41:21; 43:15;

---

[4] "Again she [Leah] conceived and bore a son, and said, 'Now this time my husband will be joined (*yillaweh*) to me, because I have borne him three sons'; therefore his name was called Levi (*lewi*)." (Gen 29:34)

44:6).[5] Only such an understanding of 14:2a fits with the statement that "aliens will join them and will cleave to the house of Jacob" (v.1b). In view of the preceding, v.2b cannot possibly be viewed as tit-for-tat retaliation. The reason is obvious. Both the captivity and the oppression of the house of Israel by the nations were the result of God's decision to punish Israel for their rebellion against him. So the nations could not be faulted, except for their arrogance in imagining that this was accomplished through their own might (10:5-19; 14:3-15). By the same token, 14:2b should be read as the second act in the plan of God who dispersed his people among the nations in order to accomplish the third act, that of gathering both his people and the nations together in his new Zion (42:1-7; 9:7).[6] Just as God took the house of Israel from Jerusalem into captivity because of—and thus away from—the idols they worshipped instead of him (10:10-11; 44:9-20; 57:3-13), so also he is taking the nations away from the deities they honored in their own countries and bringing them into his service in the new Zion. Paul vividly captured this metaphor in addressing the Gentile Corinthians and Thessalonians: "We destroy arguments and every proud obstacle to the knowledge of God, and take every thought captive to obey Christ" (2 Cor 10:5); "For they themselves report concerning us what a welcome we had among you, and how you *turned to God* from (*apo*; away from) idols, to serve a living and true God." (1 Thess 1:9) This understanding is corroborated in the final statement of Isaiah 14:2: "and rule (*radu*) over those who oppressed them (*nogsehem*)." Notice that in the previous phrase (they will bring as captives [in exile; *sobim*

---

[5] I discussed this matter in detail in conjunction with the Hivites of Gibeon who ended up as servants of the house of the Lord (Josh 9:23, 26). See *C-Josh* 144-46.
[6] See *C-Ezek* 51-52.
[7] Which is the expression of "repentance" in Pauline and Lukan terminology.

from the verb *šabah*] those who took them into exile [*šobehem*])
the author used the verb *šabah*, while here he uses two different
verbs: *radah* (rule over [as a monarch would])[8] and *nagaś*
(oppress). Although *radah* entails strictness under the rod (11:4;
Ezek 20:37; 1 Cor 4:21), its intention is to lead one's subjects on
the right path. Consequently, whereas the first "captivity" of the
house of Israel in the realm of the nations was unto punishment,
the subsequent "captivity" under the tutelage of the Law in the
new Zion is unto "security" (Is 7:9b).

The King of Babylon

In his attack on Tyre, which in his book played the role of the
quintessentially powerful nation (Ezek 26-27), Ezekiel gave
special attention to its king (28:1-19). Here Isaiah does the same
with Babylon and dedicates a lengthy passage to its king (Is 14:3-
21) cast as a satirical hymn at the occasion of his fall (vv.4b-21)
and the prelude to the end of the exile (vv.1-2). This is reflected
in the use of the verb *nuah* (rest) in the causative fifth form (give
rest): "The Lord will have compassion on Jacob and will again
choose Israel, and will set them (*hinniham*; give them rest) in
their own land (on their ground ['*adamah*])" (v.1a); "When the
Lord has given you rest (*haniah*) from your pain and turmoil and
the hard service ('*abodah qašah*) with which you were made to
serve..." (v.3) Worthy of note is the depiction of the Babylonian
exile in the same terms of "hard service" that was used to refer to

---

[8] See the classic passage Gen 1:26-28: "Then God said, 'Let us make man in our
image, after our likeness; and let them have dominion over (*yirdu*) the fish of the sea,
and over the birds of the air, and over the cattle, and over all the earth, and over every
creeping thing that creeps upon the earth.' So God created man in his own image, in
the image of God he created him; male and female he created them. And God blessed
them, and God said to them, 'Be fruitful and multiply, and fill the earth and subdue
it; and have dominion over (*redu*) the fish of the sea and over the birds of the air and
over every living thing that moves upon the earth.'"

the oppression of Israel in Egypt (Ex 1:14; 6:9). This, in turn, prepares the hearer for Isaiah's later portrayal of the return from Babylon in terms of another "exodus" (40:3; 43:16-21; 48:20-21; 51:9-11).

The taunt against the King of Babylon is dubbed *mašal*, which is the only occurrence of that noun in Isaiah; so its choice must be deliberate. *mašal* encompasses the entire gamut of the English "adage," "saying," "example," "proverb," "fable," "parable," "simile," "verisimilitude," even "story," so long as the common denominator is instruction. Put more straightforwardly, a *mašal* is "instructional" material that spans the full array from a simple statement to a full-fledged story. The scriptural Book of Proverbs, whose Hebrew title is *mišle šelomoh*, the *mešalim*[9] (plural of *mašal*) of Solomon, contains the lengthy instruction regarding the "good wife" covering 22 verses (31:10-31) as well as one verse instructional statements, and they are all *mešalim*. In our particular case here, the given *mašal* is the sad "story" of the king of Babylon who wanted to elevate himself to the rank of deity (Is 14:14) and was "brought down to the depths of the Pit" (v.15). Thus he is a prime example of the arrogance condemned in chapter 2 and, by the same token, the "oppressor" (*nogeś*; 14:4) par excellence just criticized in v.2.[10] Still there is more to the choice of *mašal* at this juncture. Since the verb *mašal* means "rule over," the King of Babylon is specifically indicted as one of the wicked "rulers" (*mošelim*) who used the "rod" (*šebet* used in 11:4) to "smite" the peoples, that is, to "rule" (*radah* used in 14:2) the nations with anger rather than with the aim of correcting their transgressions: "The Lord has broken the staff of

---

[9] Its construct state form is *mišle*, which is the form *mešalim* takes when followed by a noun complement.

[10] *nogeś* is the active participle of the verb *nagaś*.

the wicked, the scepter (*šebeṭ*; rod) of rulers (*mošelim*), that smote
the peoples in wrath with unceasing blows, that ruled (*rodeh*) the
nations in anger with unrelenting persecution." (vv.5-6)

The major criticism against the King of Babylon is that he
wanted to equal God by positioning himself not only over kings
(v.9) but also over the divine domain of the stars and the clouds
(vv.13a and 14a) in order to make himself "like the Most High
(*'elyon*)" (v.14b). His arrogance is underscored in the Hebrew
that resounds with a series of words from the root *'l(h)* connoting
ascension or height:

> You said in your heart, "I will ascend (*'e'eleh*) to heaven; above
> (*mimma'al*) the stars of God I will set my throne on high;[11] I will
> sit[12] on the mount of assembly in the far north; I will ascend
> (*'e'eleh*) above (*'al*) the heights of the clouds, I will make myself
> like the Most High (*'elyon*)." (vv.13-14)   *see OSB note- pg. 1069*

Like its counterpart "Almighty (*šadday*)" (13:6), the divine
appellation *'elyon* connotes universality. Just as was the case with
šadday, the fact that *'elyon* occurs only here in Isaiah corroborates
the deliberate use. The utter unmistakable blasphemy
perpetrated by the King of Babylon is depicted as wanting to
unseat the scriptural God both as the Lord who appeared to
Isaiah and as *'elyon* in Psalm 82:

> In the year that King Uzziah died I saw the Lord sitting (*yošeb*)
> upon (*'al*) a throne, high (*ram*) and lifted up; and his train filled
> the temple. (Is 6:1)

---

[11] The verb *'arim* (I will set on high) used here is from the same root as *ram* (high)
describing the Lord on his throne in 6:1.

[12] The verb *'ešeb* (I will sit) is from the same root as *yošeb* (sitting) describing the Lord
on his throne in 6:1.

A Psalm of Asaph. God (*'elohim*) has taken his place in the divine council (*'edah*); in the midst of the gods he holds judgment ... "I (*'ani*) say (*'amarti*; said), "You are gods, sons of the Most High (*'elyon*), all of you; nevertheless, you shall die like men, and fall like any prince." (Ps 82:1, 6-7)

You (*'attah*) said (*'amarta*) in your heart, "I will ascend to heaven; above (*mimma'al*) the stars of God (*'el*) I will set my throne (*kisse'*) on high (*'arim*); I will sit (*'eseb*) on the mount of assembly (*mo'ed*) in the far north; I will ascend above (*'al*) the heights of the clouds [of God], I will make myself like the Most High (*'elyon*)." (Is 14:13-14)

The irony is that the King of Babylon is, after all, only a "man" (Is 14:16b; see Ps 82:7) and ended "cast out, away from your sepulcher" (Is 14:19a) while "all the kings of the nations" whom he had subjugated (v.6) "lie in glory, each in his own tomb" (v.18). Moreover, in contrast with the Lord's chosen one who is likened to "a branch (*neser*) growing out of Jesse's roots" (11:1b), the King of Babylon is "cast out ... like an abominable branch (*neser*)" (14:19).[13] Finally, it is the same Lord of hosts, whose zeal will establish the throne of the new David (9:7) and keep the remnant (*se'ar*) of his people (10:20-22; 11:11, 16), who "will rise up and will cut off from Babylon name and remnant (*se'ar*), offspring and posterity" (14:22).

Before revisiting the fall of Babylon (21:1-10), the author addresses all the nations subjugated by her (14:6). The first one is Assyria (14:24-27) whose empire controlled the area before it was overwhelmed by the Babylonians. Then follow all the peoples that were under the Assyrian yoke: Philistia (vv.28-32), Moab (chs.15-16), Damascus and Israel (ch.17) who had formed

Isaiah 15

---

[13] I am following KJV that is more literal than RSV's "like a loathed untimely birth."

a coalition against Judah (7:3-9), Ethiopia (ch.18), Egypt (ch.19), and Ashdod (ch.20). The intention is clearly to present the Lord of Zion, the holy One of Israel, whose plenipotentiary emissary is Isaiah, as the God of all nations, and the only one who controls their destinies. This is evident in that in each of those oracles one hears a reference to one of his attributes or actions: ⟶ *and still does*

Assyria—The Lord of hosts has sworn: "As I have planned, so shall it be, and as I have purposed, so shall it stand, that I will break the Assyrian in my land, and upon my mountains trample him under foot." (14:24-25a)

Philistia—What will one answer the messengers of the nation? The Lord has founded Zion, and in her the afflicted of his people find refuge. (14:32)

Moab—They have sent lambs to the ruler of the land, from Sela, by way of the desert, to the mount of the daughter of Zion ... When the oppressor is no more, and destruction has ceased, and he who tramples under foot has vanished from the land, then a throne will be established in steadfast love and on it will sit in faithfulness in the tent of David one who judges and seeks justice and is swift to do righteousness. (16:1, 4b-5) *Isaiah 16*

Damascus and Israel—In that day men will regard their Maker, and their eyes will look to the Holy One of Israel; they will not have regard for the altars, the work of their hands, and they will not look to what their own fingers have made, either the Asherim or the altars of incense. (17:7-8) *Isaiah 17*

Ethiopia—At that time gifts will be brought to the Lord of hosts from a people tall and smooth, from a people feared near and far, a nation mighty and conquering, whose land the rivers divide, to Mount Zion, the place of the name of the Lord of hosts. (18:7) *Isaiah 18*

Egypt

Egypt is dealt with in a very special way. The reason is that Judah appealed to it for help against Assyria (36:6, 9) in spite of the fact that Egypt was the first place of exile for Israel; the Pharaohs who did not know Joseph (Ex 1:11-14) oppressed the people for four hundred thirty years (12:40-41). And yet, unexpectedly God decides to punish Egypt unto salvation:

> In that day the Egyptians will be like women, and tremble with fear before the hand which the Lord of hosts shakes over them … In that day there will be five cities in the land of Egypt which speak the language of Canaan and swear allegiance to the Lord of hosts. One of these will be called the City of the Sun. In that day there will be an altar to the Lord the midst of the land of Egypt, and a pillar to the Lord at its border. It will be a sign and a witness to the Lord of hosts in the land of Egypt; when they cry to the Lord because of oppressors he will send them a savior, and will defend and deliver them. And the Lord will make himself known to the Egyptians; and the Egyptians will know the Lord in that day and worship with sacrifice and burnt offering, and they will make vows to the Lord and perform them. And the Lord will smite Egypt, smiting and healing, and they will return to the Lord, and he will heed their supplications and heal them. (Is 19:16, 18-22)

Along with Egypt, salvation at the Lord's hand will also include Assyria whose punishment was mentioned earlier (14:24-27). In turn, if the Lord will eventually have pity over Israel's deadly enemies, then Israel should not lose hope in God's promise that "her iniquity is pardoned" after "she has received from the Lord's hand double for all her sins" (40:2):

> In that day there will be a highway (*mesillah*) from Egypt to Assyria, and the Assyrian will come into Egypt, and the Egyptian

[handwritten marginal note, left side:] this is very different from the OSB

[handwritten interlinear notes:] justice; judge; save; man who will save them; He will; Strike the Egyptions with a great wound and completely heal them; part

into Assyria, and the Egyptians will worship with the Assyrians. In
that day Israel will be the third with Egypt and Assyria, a blessing
in the midst of the earth, whom the Lord of hosts has blessed,
saying, "Blessed be Egypt my people, and Assyria the work of my
hands, and Israel my heritage." (19:23-25) ~~*Isaiah 19*~~

wow!

The end of the oracle concerning Egypt (vv.23-25) builds a
bridge between the promise addressed specifically to Israel
(11:11-16) and its realization in the second part of Isaiah,
namely, that the nations will join the "remnant" of Israel in
Zion, God's city restored to its original "faithfulness" (1:21a,
26b):

> In that day the Lord will extend his hand yet a second time to
> recover the remnant which is left of his people, from Assyria, from
> Egypt, from Pathros, from Ethiopia, from Elam, from Shinar,
> from Hamath, and from the coastlands (*'iyyim*; isles) of the sea.
> He will raise an ensign (*nes*) for the nations, and will assemble the
> outcasts of Israel, and gather the dispersed of Judah from the four
> corners of the earth ... And there will be a highway (*mesillah*)
> from Assyria for the remnant (*še'ar*) which is left of his people, as
> there was for Israel when they came up from the land of Egypt.
> (11:11-12, 16)

> A voice cries: "In the wilderness prepare the way of the Lord,
> make straight in the desert a highway (*mesillah*) for our God."
> (40:3)

> Go through, go through the gates, prepare the way for the people;
> build up, build up the highway (*mesillah*), clear it of stones, lift up
> an ensign (*nes*) over the peoples. (62:10)

The parallelism in phraseology is unmistakable. Besides its
occurrences in "the highway (*mesillah*) to the Fuller's Field" (Is
7:3; 36:2), *mesillah* in the singular is confined to 11:16; 19:23;
40:3; and 62:10. The phrase "ensign for the nations (over the

peoples)" in conjunction with *mesillah* is confined in Isaiah to
11:11-16 and 62:10. The "coastlands ('*iyyim*; isles)" occurs three
times in chapters 1-29 (11:11; 20:6; 24:15), yet is a staple of
chapters 40-66.

According to Genesis 10 all nations that populated the earth
after the flood came from the three sons of Noah: Shem, Ham,
and Japhet (v.1). Since Assyria derives from Shem (v.22), Egypt
from Ham (v.6), and the "coastlands of the nations"[14] (v.5a) are
associated with the descendants of Japhet (vv.2-5), one realizes
that Isaiah's phraseology is intentional; its aim is to account for
"all nations" of the earth. The mission of including all the
nations in the divine plan of salvation will devolve to the Lord's
special "servant" in Second-Isaiah (42:1-7; 49:7).

Ashdod

The message at the occasion of Ashdod's fall (ch.20) sounds out
of place especially after the oracle against Philistia (14:28-32) of
which Ashdod is a part. So the solution to understanding its
function here must lie in the wording. Let me begin with the fact
that in the entire Bible one finds the only mention of Sargon, the
Assyrian king, in Isaiah 20:1. In his Annals discovered at his
palace in Khorsabad, actual Dur-Sharrukin in Northern Iraq,
one learns extensively about his campaign in the Eastern
Mediterranean areas and especially against the city of Ashdod,
whose king fled to Ethiopia seeking help to no avail. In
retrospective, one can understand why Ethiopia is singled out
with an individualized oracle only in Isaiah (ch.18) and why the
passage 20:1-6 is brought in right after the oracles over Ethiopia
and Egypt (ch.19) and the thrice mention of them within the
chapter (20:3, 4, 5). Isaiah's special interest in Ethiopia is

---

[14] RSV has "the coastland peoples."

evidenced in the renewed singling out of that region later in the book:

> When the servants of King Hezekiah came to Isaiah, Isaiah said to them, "Say to your master, 'Thus says the Lord: Do not be afraid because of the words that you have heard, with which the servants of the king of Assyria have reviled me. Behold, I will put a spirit in him, so that he shall hear a rumor and return to his own land; and I will cause him to fall by the sword in his own land.'" The Rabshakeh returned, and found the king of Assyria fighting against Libnah; for he heard that the king had left Lachish. And when the king heard concerning Tirhakah king of Ethiopia, "Behold, he has set out to fight against you," he sent messengers again to Hezekiah, saying, "Thus shall you speak to Hezekiah king of Judah: 'Do not let your God on whom you rely deceive you by promising that Jerusalem will not be given into the hand of the king of Assyria. Behold, you have heard what the kings of Assyria have done to all lands, destroying them utterly. And shall you be delivered?'" (Is 37:5-11; see also the parallel passage 2 Kg 19:5-11).

The text clearly reflects that Hezekiah was, or at least might have been, counting on the support of the king of Ethiopia. However, the Assyrian king Hezekiah is dealing with is not Sargon, but Sennacherib (18:13; 19:16, 20, 36), which is precisely what we find later in Isaiah (36:1; 37:17, 21, 37). So one can deduce that the message of Isaiah in chapter 20 is looking to the future. This is substantiated by several features.

1. Chapter 20 is not presented as an "oracle" concerning a nation, as are the passages before and after it. It is introduced as an action taken by Isaiah in a certain historical setting, as was the case in 7:1-6. Notice, moreover, how the prophet is introduced with his full name "Isaiah the son

of Amoz" (20:2), just as was done at the beginning of each section of the book: the introduction to the entire book (1:1); the introduction to chapters 2-12 concerning Judah and Jerusalem (2:1); and the introduction to the oracles against the nations (13:1). So the author is drawing the hearer's attention to something special.

2. At no point is Ashdod the addressee; rather Isaiah's metaphoric behavior (20:2a) is "a sign and a portent against Egypt and Ethiopia" (v.2b; see also v.3).

3. The lesson is to be heeded by the anonymous "they" who "shall be dismayed and confounded because of Ethiopia their hope and of Egypt their boast" (v.4).

4. One may well surmise that, besides being historical, the choice of Ashdod was definitely made because of the meaning of the Hebrew *'ašdod* which is from the root *šdd* connoting devastation. In this manner even a hearer not acquainted with the actual events concerning the destruction of Ashdod will be struck by the futile efforts of the king of Ashdod: how can a people (notice the anonymous "they" in v.5) slated for destruction by God even hope for help and deliverance from any human source (v.6)?

So the entire passage seems to function like the message uttered by Isaiah during the time of the Assyrian hegemony (7:1-8:10) which, upon its refusal by the people (vv.11-15), was consigned as scripture for future generations (vv.16-20). Indeed, later in chapters 36-39, we shall hear that the message of Isaiah uttered under Sargon will not be heeded under Sennacherib, which will bring about the devastation of Judah by the Babylonians. Chapters 36-39 are presaged in 22:11-14, a passage leveled against Jerusalem's premature and unwarranted joy after the oracle against Babylon (21:1-10), as a reminder to the Judahites that before the fall of Babylon their city Jerusalem will be destroyed by the Babylonian king. There is clear indication that the message of 20:1-6 is intended as scripture: "at that time the Lord had spoken (*dibber*; spoke) by (*beyad*; at the hand of) Isaiah saying." (20:2) The phrase *beyad mošeh* (at the hand of Moses) as a reference to the medium through which the divine word is communicated to the people is a staple of the Books of the Law.[15] In the books of the Latter Prophets, *beyad* is used with that same connotation to reference those prophets, like Moses, who were chosen by God.[16] An example of one of these instances is important for our discussion:

> Zedekiah the son of Josiah, whom Nebuchadrezzar king of Babylon made king in the land of Judah, reigned instead of Coniah the son of Jehoiakim. But neither he nor his servants nor the people of the land listened to the words of the Lord which he spoke (*dibber*) through (*beyad*) Jeremiah the prophet. (Jer 37:1-2)

Not only did King Zedekiah, his servants, and the people not hearken to the divine message communicated through Jeremiah, but the two verses quoted above follow the lengthy chapter 36 where we hear that the words of Jeremiah were committed to writing in a scroll which King Jehoiakim shredded and burned,

---

[15] Ex 9:35; 35:29; Lev 8:36; 10:11; 26:46; Num 4:37, 45, 49; 9:23; 10:13; 15:23; 27:23; 36:13.
[16] Jer 37:2; 50:1; Hag 1:1, 3; 2:1: Zech 7:7, 12; Mal 1:1.

upon which action Jeremiah commissioned his secretary Baruch to re-write another scroll containing those same words and add to it the mention of the king's action of refusal of the message:

> And the king commanded Jerahmeel the king's son and Seraiah the son of Azriel and Shelemiah the son of Abdeel to seize Baruch the secretary and Jeremiah the prophet, but the Lord hid them. Now, after the king had burned the scroll with the words which Baruch wrote at Jeremiah's dictation, the word of the Lord came to Jeremiah: "Take another scroll and write on it all the former words that were in the first scroll, which Jehoiakim the king of Judah has burned. And concerning Jehoiakim king of Judah you shall say, 'Thus says the Lord, You have burned this scroll, saying, "Why have you written in it that the king of Babylon will certainly come and destroy this land, and will cut off from it man and beast?" Therefore thus says the Lord concerning Jehoiakim king of Judah, He shall have none to sit upon the throne of David, and his dead body shall be cast out to the heat by day and the frost by night. And I will punish him and his offspring and his servants for their iniquity; I will bring upon them, and upon the inhabitants of Jerusalem, and upon the men of Judah, all the evil that I have pronounced against them, but they would not hear.'" Then Jeremiah took another scroll and gave it to Baruch the scribe, the son of Neriah, who wrote on it at the dictation of Jeremiah all the words of the scroll which Jehoiakim king of Judah had burned in the fire; and many similar words were added to them. (36:26-32)

In Isaiah we hear a similar scenario. After Ahaz' refusal to listen to the prophet's message (chs.7-8), his son Hezekiah follows suit in refusing the now scripturalized message (20:2).[17] After relying on Egypt to help fight the Assyrian threat (36:6, 9), he goes unashamedly after Babylon to ward off a similar threat (ch.39).

---

[17] See my comments on this verse above.

This reading finds corroboration in that the parallel to the "they" addressed in the message (20:5) is "the inhabitants (*yošeb*; [the generic singular] inhabitant) of *this coastland*" (v.6). Just as was the case with the first occurrence of "coastlands (*'iyyim*; isles)" in 11:11, here also "this coastland" of Canaan is invited to look ahead to the time described in Second-Isaiah when *all* coastlands will be invited to receive the good news of liberation, together with the Judahite exiles, not so much from Assyria as from Babylon, the subjugator of Judah. That is why, although it was covered earlier in detail (13:1-14:22), the fall of Babylon is revisited in the short oracle (21:1-10) immediately following the passage concerning Ashdod.

The Sons of Ishmael

Isaiah 21-23

A further indication that the author is preparing the hearers for Second-Isaiah can be seen in the construction of the remaining chapters (21-23) of the section dealing with the nations (chs.12-23). Before dealing with Jerusalem (ch.22), the author refers to the descendants of Abraham's other sons besides Isaac (21:11-16): Dumah (v.11),[18] Dedanites (v.13),[19] Tema (v.14),[20] Kedar (vv.16-17).[21] This looks ahead toward the inclusion of all nations in the divine plan of salvation and establishment of the new Zion cast in the metaphor of Abraham whom, from one, God made into many (Is 51:1-2).

---

[18] A descendant of Ishmael (Gen 25:14).

[19] Dedan is a descendant of Keturah, Abraham's third wife (Gen 25:1-3). See also Jer 25:23; 49:8; Ezek 25:13; 27:20; 38:13.

[20] A descendant of Ishmael (Gen 25:15). See also Jer 25:23.

[21] A descendant of Ishmael (Gen 25:13). See Jer 2:10; 49:28: Ezek 27:21.

Jerusalem

If the salvation of the other nations including the coastlands as far as "the end of the earth" (42:10) is to take place after their just punishment, then the same applies to "the house of Jacob" (2:5a). That is why, after covering the children of Ishmael, the author lengthily addresses Jerusalem's premature gloating (22:1-14), which concludes with the following divine indictment:

> In that day the Lord God of hosts called to weeping and mourning, to baldness and girding with sackcloth; and behold, joy and gladness, slaying oxen and killing sheep, eating flesh and drinking wine. "Let us eat and drink, for tomorrow we die." The Lord of hosts has revealed himself in my ears: "Surely this iniquity will not be forgiven you till you die," says the Lord god of hosts. (vv.12-14)

Jerusalem is accused of having contravened the divine teaching as communicated through Isaiah. This can be detected on two levels. On the one hand, the city is dubbed twice as "the valley of vision (*ḥizzayon*)":

> The oracle concerning the valley of vision (*ḥizzayon*). What do you mean that you have gone up, all of you, to the housetops? (v.1)

> For the Lord God of hosts has a day of tumult and trampling and confusion in the valley of vision (*ḥizzayon*), a battering down of walls and a shouting to the mountains. (v.5)

By using a noun other than *ḥazon,* although from the same root, the author is drawing the hearer's attention to the fact that the false prophets of Jerusalem are not privy to the same "vision (*ḥazon*)" Isaiah "saw (*ḥazah*)"(1:1), which is nothing other than the "word" (*dabar*) that he "saw (*ḥazah*)" (2:1). On the other hand, we have a reference to a "lower pool (*berekah*)" (22:9) and an "old pool (*berekah*)" (v.11) that bring to mind the "upper pool (*berekah*)" in whose vicinity Isaiah and his son *še'ar-yašub* met Ahaz (7:3; see also 36:2).[22]

Shebna

A special case reflecting the fate of Jerusalem is illustrated through the story of the steward Shebna "who is over the household" (22:15). He is pushed aside in favor of "my [the Lord's] servant Eliakim the son of Hilkiah" (v.20) who becomes "over the household" (36:3, 22: 37:2). Nonetheless he, in turn, is dismissed (22:25). As his name suggests Eliakim (*'elyaqim*; God will raise [up]), son of Hilkiah (*ḥilqiyyahu*; the Lord has allotted, apportioned) looks like the one who will bring salvation to Jerusalem and Judah:

> … he shall be a father to the inhabitants of Jerusalem and to the house of Judah. And I shall place on his shoulder the key of the house of David; he shall open, and none shall shut; and he shall shut, and none shall open. And I will fasten him like a peg in a sure place, and he will become a throne of honor to his father's house … In that day, says the Lord of hosts, the peg that was fastened in a sure place will give way; and it will be cut down and fall, and the burden that was upon it will be cut off, for the Lord has spoken. (v.21b-22, 25)

Christ's words to Peter?

This seemingly unwarranted interest in two secondary persons of the royal court becomes understandable when one perceives their "story" as reflective of the Ahaz-Hezekiah succession. Hezekiah (*ḥizqiyyahu*: the Lord has taken control) looked at first to be the one who would "establish it [David's kingdom] and uphold it

---

[22] These instances account for all the occurrences of *berekah* in Isaiah.

with justice and with righteousness from this time forth and for evermore" (Is 9:7). This is witnessed in the description of his ascendance to the throne in the place of his father Ahaz (*'ahaz*; he took, he usurped):

> In the third year of Hoshea son of Elah, king of Israel, Hezekiah the son of Ahaz, king of Judah, began to reign. He was twenty-five years old when he began to reign, and he reigned twenty-nine years in Jerusalem. His mother's name was Abi the daughter of Zechariah. And he did what was right in the eyes of the Lord, according to all that David his father had done. He removed the high places, and broke the pillars, and cut down the Asherah. And he broke in pieces the bronze serpent that Moses had made, for until those days the people of Israel had burned incense to it; it was called Nehushtan. He trusted in the Lord the God of Israel; so that there was none like him among all the kings of Judah after him, nor among those who were before him. For he held fast to the Lord; he did not depart from following him, but kept the commandments which the Lord commanded Moses. And the Lord was with him; wherever he went forth, he prospered. He rebelled against the king of Assyria, and would not serve him. He smote the Philistines as far as Gaza and its territory, from watchtower to fortified city. (2 Kg 18:1-8)

The distance between Hezekiah and Ahaz is underscored in the name of Hezekiah's mother, Abi, daughter of Zecheriah (*zekaryah*; the Lord remembered [his promise]). It is striking, to say the least, that a woman's name would be *'abi* (my father), a shortened form of *'abiyyahu* (the Lord is my father; my father is the Lord). It is as though the author wanted to say that Hezekiah was not the son of Ahaz, but "the son of God," that is to say, the true king (Ps 2:7). And yet, later (Is 36-39), he will prove as disappointing (ch.39) as Eliakim (22:25).

Tyre

The oracle against Tyre at this juncture (ch.23) confirms that the preceding chapters look forward to Second-Isaiah. As the city that exemplifies hegemony par excellence over the Mediterranean Sea, Tyre is the prototype of all coastlands or isles. Notice how *yošeb ha'i hazzeh* (the inhabitant of *this* coast[land]) in reference to the coastal city Ashdod (20:6) becomes *yošebe 'i* (inhabitants of a [any] coast[land]), used here to reference Tyre or any coastal city in the Mediterranean all the way to Tarshish, which was allegedly the westernmost coastal city on that sea. Ships reaching or coming from it reflected richness and power, if not outright hegemony.[23] Still, even the imposing Tyre will fall:

> Wail, O ships of Tarshish, for your stronghold is laid waste. In that day Tyre will be forgotten for seventy years, like the day of one king. At the end of seventy years, it will happen to Tyre as in the song of the harlot: "Take a harp, go about the city, O forgotten harlot! Make sweet melody, sing many songs, that you may be remembered." At the end of seventy years, the Lord will visit Tyre, and she will return to her hire, and will play the harlot with all the kingdoms of the world upon the face of the earth. (23:14-17)

An attentive hearer of scripture will not miss, in these verses, the link to the fall of Babylon and the end of the exile through the thrice reference to "seventy years" (23:15 [twice], 17), which is the scriptural round figure for the period of the Babylonian exile.[24]

---

[23] 1 Kg 10:22; 22:48; Ps 48:7; 72:10; Is 2:16; 23:1, 6, 10, 14; 60:9; Jer 10:9; Ezek 27:12, 25; 38:13; Jon 1:3; 4:2.

[24] 2 Chr 36:21; Jer 25:11-12; 29:10; Dan 9:2; Zech 1:12; 7:5.

Chapter 5

God is King of Judah
and all the Nations

^{24:1}Behold, the Lord will lay waste the earth and make it desolate, and he will twist its surface and scatter its inhabitants. ²And it shall be, as with the people, so with the priest; as with the slave, so with his master; as with the maid, so with her mistress; as with the buyer, so with the seller; as with the lender, so with the borrower; as with the creditor, so with the debtor. ³The earth shall be utterly laid waste and utterly despoiled; for the Lord has spoken this word. ⁴The earth mourns and withers, the world languishes and withers; the heavens languish together with the earth. ⁵The earth lies polluted under its inhabitants; for they have transgressed the laws, violated the statues, broken the everlasting covenant. ⁶Therefore a curse devours the earth, and its inhabitants suffer for their guilt; therefore the inhabitants of the earth are scorched, and few men are left.

Isaiah 24-27

Just as is the case in Ezekiel 38-39, the function of Isaiah 24-27 after the indictment of Judah (chs.2-12) and all the nations (chs.13-23) is to hyperbolically depict God's hegemony over the entire universe.[1] As is the case in most languages, the noun "earth" (*'ereṣ*) refers to the entire orb as well as to a given area, and here in 24:1 the author uses "earth" (*'ereṣ*) to emphasize God's hegemony over all.[2] The indictment of vv.1-6 can apply to Judah, or to the Babylonian empire, or even to the entire world. Similarly, vv.7-12 can refer to Jerusalem, or Babylon, or any

---

[1] See *C-Ezek* 311-26.
[2] See similar scenarios in Ps 24; 48; 50; 58; 72; and Zeph 1:2-18.

other city. Such, in turn, underscores God's equanimity in dealing with any or all the nations of the earth.[3]

Hearing 24:1 more closely will readily show that, like all punishment before chapter 40, the act of scattering, although negative per se, aims at the ultimate action of gathering the scattered ones into one community whose members will live according to God's will on Mount Zion (24:23). Such is evident in the use of the verb *phuṣ* (scatter; v.1), which harks back to its only other occurrence in 11:12, where it is used in a context reminiscent of 2:2-4 that describes God's holy mountain Zion:

> They shall not hurt or destroy in all my holy mountain; for the earth shall be full of the knowledge of the Lord as the waters cover the sea. In that day the root of Jesse shall stand as an ensign to the peoples; him shall the nations seek, and his dwellings shall be glorious. In that day the Lord will extend his hand yet a second time to recover the remnant which is left of his people, from Assyria, from Egypt, from Pathros, from Ethiopia, from Elam, from Shinar, from Hamath, and from the coastlands of the sea. He will raise an ensign for the nations, and will assemble the outcasts of Israel, and gather the dispersed (*nephuṣot* from the verb *phuṣ*) of Judah from the four corners of the earth. (11:9-12).

The connection to chapter 11 is further sealed by the phrase "the coastlands of the sea," which is virtually confined to 11:11 and 24:15.[4]

Similarly, the following chapter (Isaiah 25) uses terminology reminiscent of Isaiah 1-12. "Faithful" (*'emunah*; 25:1) in conjunction with "city" (v.2) recalls 1:21 and 26. Care for the

---

[3] See also Amos 1-2.

[4] The only other instance of "the coastlands of the sea" is found in Esther 10:1.

poor and needy (25:4) is the opposite of the behavior of the people's leaders (1:17; 10:1-2). Those who will be saved are those who follow Isaiah's lead, waiting in hope for the realization of the word of the Lord consigned as scripture:

> The Lord spoke (*dibber*) to me again: ... "Bind up the testimony, seal the teaching among my disciples. I will wait for the Lord, who is hiding his face from the house of Jacob, and I will hope in him (*qiwwiti lo*)." (8:5, 16-17)

> He will swallow up death for ever, and the Lord God will wipe away tears from all faces, and the reproach of his people he will take away from all the earth; for the Lord has spoken (*dibber*). It will be said on that day, "Lo, this is our God; we have waited for him (*qiwwinu lo*), that he might save us. This is the Lord; we have waited for him (*qiwwinu lo*); let us be glad and rejoice in his salvation." (25:8-9)

Chapter 26 follows suit by revisiting the earlier statements concerning Samaria and Judah and applying them to the entire earth. The phrase "that the righteous (*ṣaddiq*) nation which keeps faith (*'emunim*) may enter in" (v.20) "the strong city" (v.1) recalls "the city of righteousness (*ṣedeq*), the faithful city (*ne'emanah*)" (1:26b). Again, we hear of the care for the poor and the needy within the lofty city that crushes them (26:6), and the upholding of the righteous and the upright: "The way of the righteous (*ṣaddiq*) is level (*mešarim* from *yašar* [upright, straight]); thou dost make smooth (*yašar* [upright, straight]) the path of the righteous (*ṣaddiq*)." (v.7) "Waiting for thee [the Lord] (*qiwwinuka*)" is done through following "the path of thy judgments" (vv.8-10), according to which the wicked shall be punished, and righteousness shall rule God's new Zion:

And I will restore your judges (*šopeṭim*) as at the first, and your counselors as at the beginning. Afterward you shall be called the city of righteousness, the faithful city. Zion shall be redeemed by justice (*mišpaṭ*), and those in her who repent, by righteousness. But rebels and sinners shall be destroyed together, and those who forsake the Lord shall be consumed. (1:26-28)

In the path of thy judgments (*mišpaṭim*), O Lord, we wait for thee; thy memorial name is the desire of our soul. My soul yearns for thee in the night, my spirit within me earnestly seeks thee. For when thy judgments (*mišpaṭim*) are in the earth, the inhabitants of the world learn righteousness. If favor is shown to the wicked, he does not learn righteousness; in the land of uprightness he deals perversely and does not see the majesty of the Lord. O Lord, thy hand is lifted up, but they see it not. Let them see thy zeal for thy people, and be ashamed. Let the fire for thy adversaries consume them. (26:8-11)

Moreover, the universal divine judgment will encompass all monarchs and their deities (vv.13-14; see Ps 82). Still, the most striking aspect of Isaiah 26 is the universality of the message which is reflected in the final restoration of God's "people" (*'am*; v.11) as "nation" (*goy*) and repeated for underscoring: "But thou hast increased the nation (*goy*), O Lord, thou hast increased the nation (*goy*); thou art glorified; thou hast enlarged all the borders of the land (*'ereṣ*; earth)." (v.15) The significance of that matter is that when Israel disregards God's law entrusted to it, Israel as "people laden with iniquities" becomes "a sinful nation" (1:4), that is, like any other nation that does not know that law. This, in turn, prepares for the time of restoration when Israel is slated by God himself to live with the other "nations" in the new Zion (66:18-21). That is why earlier in the chapter, which is entitled "a song that will be sung on that day in the earth [land in RSV] of Judah" (26:1) we heard that the nations are included among the righteous:

> The way of the righteous is level; thou dost make smooth the path of the righteous. In the path of thy judgments, O Lord, we wait for thee; thy memorial name is the desire of our soul. My soul yearns for thee in the night, my spirit within me earnestly seeks thee. For when thy judgments are in the earth, the inhabitants of the world (*tebel*; inhabited world)[5] learn righteousness. (vv.7-9)

Chapter 27 opens with an unequivocally universal setting in that it refers to the chaotic waters threatening the inhabited world, which forces are personified in Leviathan:[6] "In that day the Lord with his hard and great and strong sword will punish Leviathan the fleeing serpent, Leviathan the twisting serpent, and he will slay the dragon that is in the sea." (v.1) And, here again, the restoration of Jacob as the Lord's vineyard (v.2; see 5:1-7) on his holy mountain (27:13) will encompass the entire inhabited world: "In days to come Jacob shall take root, Israel shall blossom and put forth shoots, and fill the whole world (*tebel*) with fruit." (v.6)

---

[5] See my comments on Ps 93:1 in *OTI₃* 17-22.

[6] See my comments on Ps 93:3 in *OTI₃* 24-27.

Isaiah 13-23: oracles against
                          the nations

Isaiah 24-27: The Lord's hegemony
              over the entire universe

Chapter 6
God's Salvation

After the section comprising the oracles against the nations (chs.13-23) and the hailing of the Lord's hegemony over the entire universe (chs.24-27), one would expect to hear that the teaching of the divine law was being implemented in the far off coastlands as well as among the exiles of Israel (chs.40-66). However, this does not happen. Instead, the hearers have to listen to another boring and lengthy reiteration (chs.28-35) of what they already heard in chapters 1-12 concerning Ephraim and Judah, and their respective capitals Samaria and Jerusalem. The object of this is to eliminate any impression on the hearers' part that the realization of God's divine plan will take place during their lifetime, let alone any time in the foreseeable future. Between the reign of Hezekiah referred to in chapter 39 and the end of the Babylonian exile announced in chapter 40, at least 150 years will have elapsed. The message is clear: God's salvation will take place when he decides and not according to man's projections or calculations. As Jesus will later phrase it, "But of that day or that hour no one knows, not even the angels in heaven, *nor the Son*, but only the Father." (Mk 13:32) Jesus, the messenger of the same God as the prophets, is in no better position than those who were messengers before him (Heb 1:1-2). That is why there is only one course that remains for the hearers:

Take heed, watch; for you do not know when the time will come. It is like a man going on a journey, when he leaves home and puts his servants in charge, each with his work, and commands the doorkeeper to be on the watch. Watch therefore—for you do not know when the master of the house will come, in the evening, or

131

at midnight, or at cockcrow, or in the morning—lest he come suddenly and find you asleep. And what I say to you *I say to all* [subsequent generations of hearers]: Watch. (Mk 13:33-37)

In Isaiah the overwhelming power of that message is cast in a way that makes it impossible to bridge the gap between chapters 39 and 40 in one's lifetime! It is as though chapters 1-39 cover the "present" of any hearer, and chapters 40-66 describe a future beyond the hearer's grasp, a future that is always to "come," and is forever a reminder that the prophetic message addressed to "us" always encompasses all others, including those in the far off lands whom we may not even be aware of. The Apostle Paul will take this matter seriously:

In Christ Jesus, then, I have reason to be proud of my work for God. For I will not venture to speak of anything except what Christ has wrought through me to win obedience from the Gentiles, by word and deed, by the power of signs and wonders, by the power of the Holy Spirit, so that from Jerusalem and as far round as Illyricum I have fully preached the gospel of Christ, thus making it my ambition to preach the gospel, not where Christ has already been named, lest I build on another man's foundation, but as it is written, "They shall see who have never been told of him, and they shall understand who have never heard of him." This is the reason why I have so often been hindered from coming to you. (Rom 15:17-22)

The Romans listening to that letter addressed to them will have heard Paul's voice without having seen his face, which they possibly may not ever get to behold, unless God wills it (vv.30-32). This is what scripture is all about: hearing God's voice without ever being privy to beholding his face since he has no statue! In other words, unlike other deities, the scriptural God is tantamount to an exclusive parental voice that ever leads us on the right path toward the new Zion.

Isaiah 28

God's Word concerning Samaria

In order to remind the hearers that Samaria shall not be forgotten, the author revisits in detail the sins of Samaria (ch.28) as he had done earlier in 9:7-10:4.[1] The close link between these two passages is secured through the phrase "the remnant (which is left) of his people" in reference to Samaria (11:11, 16; 28:5) as well as through the mention of its leaders' arrogance (9:8-9; 28:1-4) resulting in their misleading the people (9:13-15; 10:1-2; 28:7). As was explained earlier in chapter 2, such arrogance is not a "vice," rather it is a revolt against the only master, with the aim of taking his place of honor. And again, just as in chapter 2, divine judgment will consist in reversing that attempt:

> [28:1]Woe to the proud crown (*'ateret ge'ut*) of the drunkards of Ephraim, and to the fading flower of its glorious beauty (*ṣebi tiph'arto*), which is on the head of the rich valley of those overcome with wine! [2]Behold, the Lord has one who is mighty and strong; like a storm of hail, a destroying tempest, like a storm of mighty, overflowing waters, he will cast down to the earth with violence. [3]The proud crown (*'ateret ge'ut*) of the drunkards of Ephraim will be trodden under foot; [4]and the fading flower of its glorious beauty (*ṣebi tiph'arto*), which is on the head of the rich valley, will be like a first-ripe fig before the summer: when a man sees it, he eats it up as soon as it is in his hand. [5]In that day the Lord of hosts will be a crown of glory (*'ateret ṣebi*), and a diadem of beauty (*ṣephirat tiph'arah*), to the remnant of his people; [6]and a spirit of justice to him who sits in judgment, and strength to those who turn back the battle at the gate.

---

[1] See also Ezekiel 16:46-55; 23:4-10, 33-34; 37:15-28, and my comments thereon in *C-Ezek*.

The punishment of the leaders will consist in their being snared by their own stratagem. On the day of judgment they will be reminded word for word (vv.10 and 13)[2] of the divine requests that recently weaned children (v.9), nay, even people of strange language (v.11) would have easily understood.[3] The original Hebrew of v.10 and 13 reflects that God's words are spelled out one at a time, the message being "this is rest (*menuhah*), [that you] give rest (*hanihu*) to the weary," "yet they would not hear" (v.12). The importance of this teaching will be fully revealed at the beginning of the concluding chapter 66 where we encounter the only other occurrence of "rest" (*menuhah*) in the singular in Isaiah: "Thus says the Lord: 'Heaven is my throne and the earth is my footstool; what is the house which you would build for me, and what is the place of my rest (*menuhah*)? All these things my hand has made, and so all these things are mine, says the Lord. But this is the man to whom I will look, he that is humble and contrite in spirit, and trembles at my word.'" (vv.1-2).

The common fate of Samaria and Jerusalem is sealed in the sudden shift to Jerusalem in 28:24 which is no less than a concluding statement to the preceding: "*Therefore* hear the word of the Lord, you scoffers, who rule this people in Jerusalem!" This is done in view of the mention of (the new) Zion that will

---

[2] "For it is precept upon precept, precept upon precept, line upon line, line upon line, here a little, there a little ... Therefore the word of the Lord will be to them precept upon precept, precept upon precept, line upon line, line upon line, here a little, there a little."

[3] Compare with Ezek 3:4-7 (And he said to me, "Son of man, go, get you to the house of Israel, and speak with my words to them. For you are not sent to a people of foreign speech and a hard language, but to the house of Israel— not to many peoples of foreign speech and a hard language, whose words you cannot understand. Surely, if I sent you to such, they would listen to you. But the house of Israel will not listen to you; for they are not willing to listen to me; because all the house of Israel are of a hard forehead and of a stubborn heart.")

encompass both Samaria and Jerusalem and will be built on "a stone, a tested stone, a precious cornerstone, of a sure foundation" (v.16) which earlier functioned as "a stone of offense, and a rock of stumbling *to both houses of Israel,* a trap and a snare to the inhabitants of Jerusalem" (8:14).[4] This reversal of fate, described as "strange" and "alien," is further underscored in the reference to God's judgment against his people in terms of two previous interventions on their behalf: "For the Lord will rise up as on Mount Perazim, he will be wroth as in the valley of Gibeon; to do his deed—strange is his deed! and to work his work—alien is his work!" (v.21) Gibeon and the valley of Aijalon are the site of Joshua's victory over the Amorites (Josh 10:12-13), whereas Perazim is linked to the defeat of the Philistines at David's hand (2 Sam 5:19-20), in both cases with express divine approval.

Isaiah 29

Ariel - 3 meanings

God's Word concerning Jerusalem

Beginning with chapter 29, the rest of the section (chs.28-35) deals with Jerusalem, in preparation for chapters 36-39. The city is addressed as Ariel (*'ari'el*), which use is exclusive to this chapter (29:1 [twice], 2[twice], 7). This name is chosen to function in three different ways at the same time. The three instances of the noun *'ari'el* in Ezekiel 43:15 [twice] and 16 refer to the altar hearth where sacrifices are slaughtered or burnt. Such fits the context of Isaiah 29:1-2 where reference is made to the annual feasts when offerings are made, which are loathed by God (1:11-15; see also 66:3-4) and for which Jerusalem will be made into an Ariel (Is 29:2b), that is to say, will be burned down in a siege (1) (vv.3-8) orchestrated by God himself (v.3a; see also Ezek 4:1-3).

---

[4] The intended link between these two passages is sealed in that they virtually account for all the rare instances of the singular "stone" (*'eben*) in Isaiah. Its only other occurrence is in the pair "wood and stone" in reference to the idols (37:19).

The other meaning of Ariel that also fits the context is "God (*'el*) is a lion (*'ari*)," as he will be described later in 38:13, with a view to the fact that, as a lion, God could fight for Zion, should he decide to save it (31:4). After all Zion is his city; he punishes her when she plays the unfaithful harlot (1:21-25), then redeems her (vv.26-27). The last and most pertinent connotation of Ariel is "God is my light." The house of Jacob was supposed to "walk in that light" (2:5), yet did not, and so it was destroyed by that same light (vv.6-21). In those times, fire *was* light and light *was* fire. God's light will keep burning Jerusalem until she decides to "walk" by it.

Chapters 29-35 not only deal with Jerusalem but also look ahead to the second part of the book and hark back to chapters 1-12 as well. The vocabulary and phraseology bridge these two sections of Isaiah. Here are some of the most prominent features:

1. With the exceptions of 17:7 and 37:23 the phrase "the holy One of Israel" occurs at a high incidence in chapters 1-12, 29-31, and 40-66.[5]

2. The reference to Abraham is confined to 29:22; 41:8; 51:2; and 63:16.

3. The verb *padah* (redeem; ransom) occurs only in 1:27; 29:22; 35:10; and 51:11. In the last two instances we actually have the same sentence word for word: "And the ransomed (*peduye*) of the Lord shall return, and come to Zion with singing; everlasting joy shall be upon their heads;

---

[5] 1:4; 5:19, 24; 10:20; 12:6; 29:19, 23; 30:11, 12, 15; 31:1; 41:14, 16, 20; 43:3, 14; 45:11; 47:4; 48:17; 49:7 [twice]; 54:5; 55:5; 60:9, 14 [in conjunction with Zion as the City of the Lord].

they shall obtain joy and gladness, and sorrow
and sighing shall flee away."

4. The reference to the ransomed as Abraham's or
   God's children as well as "the work of my [the
   Lord's] hands" occurs only in 29:23 and 45:11 in
   conjunction with "the Holy One of Israel/Jacob":
   "For when he [Abraham] sees his children, the
   work of my hands (*ma'aśeh yaday*), in his midst,
   they will sanctify my name; they will sanctify the
   Holy One of Jacob, and will stand in awe of the
   God of Israel"; "Thus says the Lord, the Holy
   One of Israel, and his Maker: 'Will you question
   me about my children (*banay*; my sons), or
   command me concerning the work of my hands
   (*po'al yaday*)?'"

5. The verb *ḥabaš* (bind up [a wound]) is found
   only in 1:6; 30:26; and 61:1.

6. Finally the root *ga'al* which is trademark of
   chapters 40-66 occurs elsewhere in the book only
   in 35:9 to speak of the "redeemed" (*ge'ulim*).

In my revised first volume of Introduction to the Old
Testament I argue that Ezekiel is the "father of scripture" and
that the Book of Ezekiel and Isaiah 40-66 form the core around
which the entire scripture revolves.[6] In this regard it is interesting
to note that many features of Isaiah 29-35, which prepare for the
second part of the book, are essential components of the
Ezekelian message. I should like to underscore five of those
features:

---

[6] *OTI₁* 29-40.

1. The criticism of the reliance on Egypt. The importance given this teaching is evident in its repetition (Is 30:1-5 and 31:1-3, compare with Ezek 29-32).[7]

    against → the current administration (Ahaz et al)

    Isaiah 30-31

2. The anti-David stance in view of the everlasting covenant with the new David (Is 55:3: compare with Ezek 34:25; 37:26). Notice how Ariel that is criticized is presented as "the city where David encamped" as a king would with his army. Notice also that the new Zion will be a city where "the eyes of the blind shall be opened ... then shall the lame man leap like a hart" (35:5a, 6a; see also 29:18 and 33:23), whereas blind and lame were excised out of the "city of David" (2 Sam 5:6-9).

    35

3. The new David will be a shepherd just as is his God: God's rule will be implemented in a pasture land for shepherds rather than in fortified kingly cities (Ezek 34).[8] We find an echo of such teaching in Isaiah 33 where the new Zion is described thus: "Look upon Zion, the city of our appointed feasts! Your eyes will see Jerusalem, a quiet habitation (*naweh*; pasture), an immovable tent (*'ohel*), whose stakes will never be plucked up, nor will any of its cords be broken." (v.20)

    Isaiah 33

4. In turn this pasture is the result of the outpouring of the divine spirit (32:15-20) which

    Isaiah 32

---

[7] See my comments in *C-Ezek.*

[8] See my comments on that chapter in *C-Ezek* 299-310 where I underscore its anti-kingly stand in favor for the pasture land of a shepherd's flock.

is both reminiscent of Ezekiel 37:1-14 as well as of Isaiah 11:1-9 and looks ahead to the second part of the book (42:1; 44:3; 59:21; 61:1; 63:14).

5. Finally, and most importantly, is the consignment of Isaiah's message into a "book" for the future generations: "Seek and read from the book (*sepher*; scroll) of the Lord: Not one of these shall be missing; none shall be without her mate. For the mouth of the Lord has commanded, and his Spirit has gathered them." (34:16; compare with Ezek 2:9-3:3 and also Is 8:16-20).

Isaiah 34

The Disobedience of the House of David

Isaiah 36-39

The function of chapters 36-39 is to underscore that the message of Isaiah to Ahaz and to the house of David (7:2, 13) was ultimately not heeded. Not only did Ahaz try to use God's concern for Jerusalem to his own advantage, his son Hezekiah did the same. The intended parallelism between Ahaz and Hezekiah is evident in that the Lord offers a sign (*'ot*) that he would save Jerusalem (7:11; 37:30) to both of them. After having heard the prophet's caveat against appealing to Egypt for help against Assyria (30:1-7; 31:1-3), the hearers cannot be but struck at that, even after his alleged repentance (38:9-20) upon being healed from a mortal sickness (vv.1-8), Hezekiah still shamelessly (vv.5-7) tried to enlist the help of Babylon (39:1-2).

O Lord have mercy on us!

The announcement to Isaiah that the Judahite kings were relegated to a position of figurehead (6:1) is transparent in chapters 36-39. God never addresses Hezekiah except through the intermediacy of the prophet Isaiah (37:6-7, 21; 38:1; 39:5-7); conversely, Hezekiah enquires of God via Isaiah (37:5). Once

Hezekiah has uttered his last words (39:9) he is consigned to oblivion. It is only Isaiah's *voice* that will resound through the rest of the book (chs.40-66) on behalf of the Lord, the "King of Israel" (41:21; 43:15; 44:6). Even the name Isaiah is not to be found in those chapters; only his voice will be heard. Ironically, as we shall see, God, who has dismissed the kingship of Judah as invalid, will further stun the hearers by choosing Cyrus, the king of a foreign nation, as *his* shepherd (44:28) and *his* anointed (45:1).

Part II

Isaiah Chapters 40-55

Chapter 7
The Divine Word

The Word of God

When Second-Isaiah (chs.40-55) is heard in tandem with the first part of the book, its function becomes clear: "the word" communicated to Isaiah (2:1) and consigned in a book (8:16-20; 29:11-12, 18; 30:8; 34:16) is realized as promised in spite of the lull of over 150 years between chapters 39 and 40. An overview of the use of the noun *dabar* (word) and the verb *dibber* (speak) will confirm this thesis. First and foremost, the divine word brackets Second-Isaiah as an *inclusio*:

> The grass withers, the flower fades, when the breath of the Lord blows upon it; surely the people is grass. The grass withers, the flower fades; but the word of our God will stand for ever. (40:7-8)

> For as the rain and the snow come down from heaven, and return not thither but water the earth, making it bring forth and sprout, giving seed to the sower and bread to the eater, so shall my word be that goes forth from my mouth; it shall not return to me empty, but it shall accomplish that which I purpose, and prosper in the thing for which I sent it. (55:10-11)

In both these cases, what is underscored is the assurance of that word's efficacy, despite its refusal by the people and the lengthy lapse of time between its issuance and its implementation.

Furthermore, the occurrences of the root *dbr* throughout chapters 40-55 will follow a programmatic sequence:

1. Just as First-Isaiah is entitled as "word" (2:1), so also the message of Second-Isaiah is introduced

with the summons "Speak (*dabberu*) tenderly to Jerusalem" (40:2).

2. The word of the Lord that stands forever (40:8), and which is a word of good tidings (v.9), is not communicated through any potential "counselor" save Isaiah. First in 41:27-28 we are told: "I first have declared it to Zion, and I give to Jerusalem a herald of good tidings. But when I look there is no one; among these there is no counselor (*yo'es*) who, when I ask, gives an answer (*dabar*, word)." Yet, the following instance of *dabar* refers clearly to Isaiah who had been introduced earlier (20:3) as "my servant': "[I am the Lord] who confirms the word (*dabar*) of his servant, and performs the counsel ('*asah*; from the same root as *yo'es*) of his messengers; who says of Jerusalem, 'She shall be inhabited,' and of the cities of Judah, 'They shall be built, and I will raise up their ruins'." (44:26)

3. Because the Lord has spoken his word through Isaiah, a word that was consigned in writing, he can boast that (a) he spoke it "openly" for all to hear (45.19);[1] (b) he committed himself to its realization (v.23);[2] and (c) he shall make sure that the word he has spoken "from of old," that is to

---

[1] I did not speak (*dibbarti*) in secret, in a land of darkness; I did not say to the offspring of Jacob, "Seek me in chaos." I the Lord speak (*dober*) the truth, I declare what is right.

[2] By myself I have sworn, from my mouth has gone forth in righteousness a word (*dabar*) that shall not return: "To me every knee shall bow, every tongue shall swear."

say, before either Cyrus or the exiles were even born, will come to pass (46:8-11)③

4. The Lord's servant, Jacob, was punished into exile because of his disobedience (42:18-25). In order to save the remnant of that servant, God chooses a new servant, Cyrus, for this mission (44:24-28). The calling of Cyrus is done through a word: "I have spoken (*dibbarti*)" (48:15, 16) "from the beginning" and "not in secret" (v.16).

5. However, beyond Cyrus, whose special mission is only toward the children of Jacob, God already has in mind choosing a servant whose mission is to the nations, among whom is Cyrus himself, as well as to the remnant of Jacob (42:1-13; 49:1-7). The distinctiveness of his mission lies in that he will be directly taught by God (50:4b-5) and will carry his "word" (*dabar*) to sustain "him that is weary" (v.4a) and all those who would "obey his [the servant's] voice" (v.10).

6. Before the last instance of the root *dbr* in 55:11, it occurs in 51:16 in conjunction with "my [God's] words" entrusted to Israel in the Law. "I have put my words in your mouth" (51:16) recalls "For this commandment which I command you this day is not too hard for you,

---

③ Remember this and consider, recall it to mind, you transgressors, remember the former things of old; for I am God, and there is no other; I am God, and there is none like me, declaring the end from the beginning and from ancient times things not yet done, saying, "My counsel (*'asah*) shall stand, and I will accomplish all my purpose," calling a bird of prey from the east, the man of my counsel (*'asah*) from a far country. I have spoken (*dibbarti*), and I will bring it to pass; I have purposed, and I will do it.

neither is it far off ... But the word (*dabar*) is very near you; it is in your mouth and in your heart, so that you can do it" (Deut 30:11, 14). It is precisely Israel's breaking of that covenant that necessitated the new "word" consigned in Isaiah 40-55 (55:11).

The breaking of the covenant is an essential component of the message of Second-Isaiah, This is evident in the opening verse where the announcement of the consolation is intertwined with reference to the preceding punishment: "Comfort, comfort my people, says your God. Speak tenderly to Jerusalem, and cry to her that her warfare is ended, that her iniquity is pardoned, that she has received from the Lord's hand double for all her sins." (40:1-2) Furthermore, as we shall see throughout the following chapters, Israel is repeatedly reminded of its blindness and deafness to God's teaching. It is precisely this reminder of the sin of Israel, which occasioned the punishment into exile, that builds the bridge between First-Isaiah and Second-Isaiah. It is the same Lord who issued through his same word both the indictment and the hope of restoration. That word is the one inscribed in the "book of the Lord" (34:16) at the hand of Isaiah, written for the yet unborn generations (8:16-20). Even now after generations of the people have died, just as "the grass withers and the flower fades" (40:7), "the word of our God is still standing" (v.8). And just as Ezekiel taught (ch.34), upon his redeeming his people, God will be their King (Is 41:21; 43:15; 44:6) who "comes with might, and his arm rules for him" (40:10). Nevertheless, he "will feed his flock like a shepherd, he will gather the lambs in his arms, he will carry them in his bosom, and gently lead those that are with young" (v.11). The intentionality of this imagery is evident in that (1) this is the only reference to God as shepherd in Isaiah, and (2) the only other instance of shepherd in the book is made in conjunction with King Cyrus "my shepherd" (44:28) "whose right hand I [the Lord] have grasped, to subdue nations before him and ungird the loins of kings, to open doors before him that gates may not be closed" (45:1). That is why, the new Zion, though depicted as a city in Isaiah, is nothing other than the city Ezekiel refers to as "the Lord is there" (48:35b), around which extends a pasture land without cities (vv.1-35a). The parallelism between Isaiah and Ezekiel is confirmed in that the new David, referred to in Ezekiel 37 as shepherd and through whom God establishes a "covenant of peace" with his flock, appears in the closing chapter of Second-Isaiah—which is the sole reference to David in chapters 40-66—in these terms: "Incline your ear, and come to me; hear, that your soul may live; and I will make with you an everlasting covenant, my steadfast, sure love for David ... For you shall go out in joy, and be led forth in peace; the mountains and the hills before you shall break forth into singing, and all the trees of the field shall clap their hands." (55:3, 12) The importance of the metaphor of shepherd to speak of God the redeemer finds corroboration in that it is not only encountered in Isaiah and Ezekiel, but it is also found in the other two volumes of the latter Prophets, Jeremiah (31:10) and the scroll of the Twelve (Mic 7:14).

The Lord is the Universal God

Standard protocol is that a monarch is chosen by its nation's deity, rather than by a foreign deity. In order to prepare for God's choice of Cyrus in 41:1-5, the author introduces the Lord as the universal and sole valid God in a very extensive fashion:

Who has measured the waters in the hollow of his hand and marked off the heavens with a span, enclosed the dust of the earth in a measure and weighed the mountains in scales and the hills in a balance? Who has directed the Spirit of the Lord, or as his counselor has instructed him? Whom did he consult for his enlightenment, and who taught him the path of justice, and taught him knowledge, and showed him the way of understanding? Behold the nations are like a drop from a bucket, and are accounted as the dust on the scales; behold he takes up the isles like fine dust ... All the nations are as nothing before him, they are accounted by him as less than nothing and emptiness. To whom then will you liken God, or what likeness compare with him? ... It is he who sits above the circle of the earth, and its inhabitants are like grasshoppers; who stretches out the heavens like a curtain, and spreads them like a tent to dwell in; who brings princes to nought, and makes the rulers of the earth as nothing. Scarcely are they planted, scarcely shown, scarcely has their stem taken root in the earth when he blows upon them, and they wither, and the tempest carries them off like stubble. To whom then will you compare me, that I should be like him? says the Holy One ... Why do you say, O Jacob, and speak, O Israel, "My way is hid from the Lord, and my right is disregarded by my God"? Have you not known? Have you not heard? The Lord is the everlasting God, the Creator of the ends of the earth. He does not faint or grow weary, his understanding is unsearchable. (40:12-15, 17-18, 22-25, 27-28)

The aim of 40:12-31 is to overwhelm the hearers with this new reality, namely, that the Lord is the God of all nations (vv.15, 17). However, the nations are immediately equated with the isles (*'iyyim*; coastlands, v.15). That this matter is given importance is evident in v.12 where the waters are the first element in the "world" God rules over. The significance given *'iyyim*[4] is further confirmed in that they are the main target of the message in the missions of both servants of the Lord: the humble servant (42:4, 10, 12, 15; see also 49:1) as well as the mighty Cyrus (41:1, 5). The universality of God is further detected in 40:23 that recalls

---

[4] See my earlier comments in conjunction with 11:11.

Psalm 82 where God judges all the deities of the earth. Still, his universality does not affect his ultimate attribute of a shepherd who will bring salvation to both the nations and the sons of Jacob. This is substantiated in that his dwelling is likened to a "tent" (40:22), just as the new Zion was viewed earlier (33:20). Another indication of God's universality is that in 40:25 he is referred to simply as "the Holy One" instead of the usual "the Holy One of Israel." However his holiness is revealed specifically in the Law he gave to Israel; that is why Israel is reprimanded in these terms: "Why do you say, O Jacob, and speak, O Israel, 'My way (*derek*) is hid from the Lord, and my right (*mišpaṭ*; justice) is disregarded by my God'? Have you not known? Have you not heard?" (vv.27-28a)[5] Such disregard for the divine law was essentially the "sin" for which the sons of Jacob ended doubly punished (v.1). Yet, there is hope for those "who wait for (*qoyim*) the Lord," which hope will be realized (49:23) through the mission of the servant of the Lord (vv.1-7) whom the Holy One of Israel will eventually choose:

> Thus says the Lord, the Redeemer of Israel and his Holy One, to one deeply despised, abhorred by the nations, the servant of rulers: "Kings shall see and arise; princes, and they shall prostrate themselves; because of the Lord, who is faithful, the Holy One of Israel, who has chosen you." (v.7)

> Kings shall be your foster fathers, and their queens your nursing mothers. With their faces to the ground they shall bow down to you, and lick the dust of your feet. Then you will know that I am the Lord; those who wait for (*qoyim*) me shall not be put to shame. (v.23)

---

[5] *derek* and *mišpaṭ* are specifically legal terminology.

The Redemption of Israel

After a brief mention of how God will implement his plan of salvation through Cyrus (41:1-5), which will be developed later (44:24-45:7), the author reminds the hearers that it is the Lord who will be behind the salvation of Israel, albeit at Cyrus' hand. This is done on two levels. First, Israel is described as the chosen servant whom God alone sustains (41:8-11), and he commits himself to be its "redeemer" (*go'el*; v.14). The importance of the root *g'l* is reflected in its high incidence in Second-Isaiah, both in the participial form *go'el* (41:14; 43:14; 44:6, 24; 47:4; 48:17; 49:7, 26; 54:5, 8) and the verbal form *ga'al* (43:1; 44:22, 23; 48:20; 52:3). In ancient Hebrew society, a man may be forced to sell his property or even sell himself into slavery to pay a debt. His "redeemer" was generally his closest kin whose duty was to buy back the sold property or purchase the man's freedom in order to preserve the family and its property intact.[6] Rigid rules required that if a distant relative wished to act as the redeemer he would have to have the permission of the rightful one. Conversely, it was considered shameful for the closest relative to refuse to fulfill what was not only a right but a duty. Thus, in proclaiming himself as Israel's *go'el* the Lord was reminding both Israel and the nations that he had not forfeited that right. Despite what either group might be inclined to think, God was determined to exercise his right to keep Israel within his own sphere of influence and not allow it to be alienated, either by others or even by itself. Essentially, Second-Isaiah is rendering in positive terms what Ezekiel expressed negatively as an invective against Israel: both

---

[6] See Lev 25:25-33, 48-55; see also 27:16-33. The *go'el* also bore a responsibility to father children for a man who had died without an heir, again in order to preserve the family (Deut 25:5-10; Gen 38), and if the man had been murdered, the *go'el haddam* (redeemer of blood) would avenge the crime (Num 35:19-27). The best example of the rules of redemption in actual practice is in Ruth (3:9, 12; and especially 4:1-15).

prophets stress God's unimpeachable rule over Israel and his prerogative to "make woe or make weal" (Is 45:7) as he sees fit. In other words, Israel may refuse to accept God's salvation, but it cannot decide not to let him save! He will not allow Israel to make him appear to others as if he were in fact not a *go'el,* a redeeming and saving God.[7] In turn, this functional uniqueness of Israel's deity is underscored in 41:8-20, which is flanked by a sarcastic aside (vv.6-7) and a full-fledged belittling irony (21-29) against the other deities depicted as idols fabricated by human hands.

---

[7] See 42:18-25; 48:1-11, 16-19.

1. 42:1-7
2. 49:1-7
3. 50:4-10
4. 52:13-53:12

Chapter 8

The Servant Poems

The First Servant Poem

^{42:1}Behold my servant, whom I uphold, my chosen, in whom my soul delights; I have put my Spirit upon him, he will bring forth justice to the nations. ²He will not cry or lift up his voice, or make it heard in the street; ³a bruised reed he will not break, and a dimly burning wick he will not quench; he will faithfully bring forth justice. ⁴He will not fail or be discouraged till he has established justice in the earth; and the coastlands wait for his law. ⁵Thus says God, the Lord, who created the heavens and stretched them out, who spread forth the earth and what comes from it, who gives breath to the people upon it and spirit to those who walk in it: ⁶"I am the Lord, I have called you in righteousness, I have taken you by the hand and kept you; I have given you as a covenant to the people, a light to the nations, ⁷to open the eyes that are blind, to bring out the prisoners from the dungeon, from the prison those who sit in darkness. (42:1-7)

After the teaching regarding the redeemer is established, the hearers are ready for the passage that introduces, for the first time, the "unnamed" servant of the Lord (vv.1-4). What is unique about this servant is not that God upholds him, or chooses him, or delights in him, or puts his spirit upon him, nor even that his mission is to administer justice. One or more of these characteristics are also found in divinely appointed persons, such as the king, a priest, or a prophet. What is particular to this servant is that he will bring forth the divine *mišpaṭ* (justice, [just] judgment) not just to Israel but also *to the nations*. The centrality of this thought in the author's mind can be confirmed by its

153

repetition in vv.3c and 4bc,[1] and especially by the fact that this sets up an *inclusio*[2] with v.1d. More specifically, the *inclusio* is formed by vv.1d and 3c, since the two lines are virtually identical in both wording and structure:

> *mišpaṭ laggoyim yoṣeh* (v.1d)
>> (just) judgment to the nations he will bring forth
> *le'emet yoṣeh mišpaṭ* (v.3c)
>> faithfully/truthfully[3] he will bring forth (just) judgment

These lines bracket a well-knit passage written according to the rules of poetic synonymic parallelism[4] as well as inversion.[5] Not only are vv.2 and 3ab composed of two lines forming a synonymic parallel, but the entire section (vv.1d-3) forms an inversion of the ABB'A' pattern: v.1d (A), v.2 (B), v.3ab (B'), v.3c (A'). The paradoxical message conveyed in this passage is that the servant will carry out his kingly role of implementing God's *mišpaṭ* without using the corresponding royal instruments

---

[1] The word *torah* ([just] law/instruction) is parallel in meaning to *mišpaṭ*.

[2] An *inclusio* (Latin, meaning "inclusion") is a device according to the scheme A...A' whereby the main thought opens as well as concludes a passage, bracketing the entire passage. Its purpose is to clearly indicate to the hearer or reader the main thought or subject matter of the passage.

[3] Literally, "to/unto faithfulness/truth." Notice the parallelism in Hebrew due to the use of the same preposition *l* (to) before "nations" in v.1d and "faithfulness/truth" in v.3c.

[4] Synonymic parallelism is a literary device whereby each verse consists of two lines which are parallel in that they express the same thought using different words. Psalm 51 provides an obvious and well-known example: "Have mercy on me, O God, according to thy steadfast love; according to thy abundant mercy blot out my transgressions. Wash me thoroughly from my iniquity, and cleanse me from my sin! For I know my transgressions, and my sin is ever before me." (vv.1-3) Another example is Amos 2:6b: "because they sell the righteous for silver and the needy for a pair of shoes."

[5] An inversion follows the pattern ABB'A' in which each letter and its correspondent refer to the same or similar item or thought. One can find a clear example in Jesus' famous saying: "For whoever would *save his life* (A) will *lose it* (B); and whoever *loses his life* (B') for my sake and the gospel's will *save it* (A')." (Mk 8:35).

of power—the spoken word and the iron rod.[6] A stranger turn of events can hardly be imagined: the Lord's servant will implement the divine *mišpaṭ* among the nations not by rewarding good and punishing evil but by remaining passive—by doing nothing!

This interpretation is corroborated by the wording of v.4 which informs us that he will not *yikheh* (fail, burn dimly) and he will not *yaruṣ* (be discouraged, bruised), using the same verbs which in v.3 describe respectively the wick he will not quench (v.3b) and the reed he will not break (v.3a).[7] Thus, not only will the servant be inactive, but his behavior seems to be connected with some kind of pressure or difficulty or persecution he will have to suffer. In other words, *silence* and *suffering* are the paradoxical trademarks of this divine messenger in the implementation of a "kingly" mission which would entail divine utterance and divine victory.[8] The paradox is all the more stunning when one takes into consideration that the basic mission of this servant in Second-Isaiah is to bring God's *mišpaṭ* to the nations in order to show that he is the one universal God controlling the destinies of both Israel and the nations.

But what exactly does "*mišpaṭ* among the nations" mean? A solid starting point for an investigation into the significance of this phrase would be v.4c, where the terms "earth" and "coastlands" parallel "nations" in v.1d. "Earth" is too general a word to yield any help, but usage of *'iyyim* (coastlands/islands) in

---

[6] Compare this with the messianic prophecy in Is 11:3-4.

[7] The intended parallelism is further underscored by the inversion pattern: *raṣuṣ* (bruised; passive participle of the verb *raṣaṣ*; v.3a), *kehah* (dimly burning; derived from the verb *kahah*; v.3b), *yikheh* (imperfect of *kahah*; v.4aa), *yaruṣ* (imperfect of *raṣaṣ*; v.4ab). Even if *yaruṣ* is the imperfect of *ruṣ* (to flee/run away), the effect will still be the same.

[8] Compare with Cyrus who is granted victory over the nations when acting on behalf of the Lord (45:1-7).

Second-Isaiah is more specific and relatively restricted. Yet from its use in Isaiah and from other Old Testament texts one can easily gather that *'iyyim* are stretches of land bordering on or surrounded by water[9] and thus are to be understood as coastlands or islands. In the mind of the ancient Israelite or Judahite such lands represent the far ends of the earth[10] or the (other) peoples or nations.[11] When *'iyyim* is not qualified by the name of a specific nation, it connotes *all* the nations, as far as the ends of the earth. In returning to the occurrences of this word in Second-Isaiah, we find that most of them appear in conjunction with *mišpaṭ*.[12]

1   Whom did he consult for his enlightenment, and taught him the path of justice (*mišpaṭ*), and taught him knowledge, and show him the way of understanding. Behold, the nations are like a drop from a bucket, and are accounted as dust on the scales; behold he takes up the isles like fine dust. (40:14-15)

2   Listen to me in silence, O coastlands; let the peoples renew their strength; let them approach, then let them speak; let us together draw near for judgment (*mišpaṭ*). (41:1)

3   He will not fail or be discouraged till he has established justice (*mišpaṭ*) in the earth; and the coastlands wait for his law. (42:4)

4   Listen to me, O coastlands, and hearken you peoples from afar. The Lord called me from the womb, and from the body of my mother he named my name. He made my mouth like a sharp

---

[9] See especially 42:10, 15; see also 11:11; 24:15; Esth 10:1.

[10] See 41:5; 42:10; 49:1. See also 66:19; Ps 97:1; Jer 31:10.

[11] See 40:15; 41:1; 42:11-12; 51:4-5. See also Gen 10:5; Jer 2:10; 47:4; Ezek 27:6-7; Zeph 2:11 ("lands" in RSV).

[12] 5 out of 9 (or 5 out of 7 if one counts the pairs in 41:1 and 5, and in 42:10 and 12, as single instances of each). Note that RSV translates *mišpaṭ* variously in these texts as "judgment," or "justice," or "right."

sword, in the shadow of his hand he hid me; he made me a polished arrow and in his quiver he hid me away. And he said to me, "You are my servant, Israel, in whom I will be glorified." (49:1-3)

5 Listen to me, my people, and give ear to me, my nation; for a law will go forth from me, and my justice (*mišpaṭ*) for a light to the peoples. My deliverance draws near speedily, my salvation has gone forth, and my arms will rule (*yišpoṭu*; will rule justly) the peoples; the coastlands wait for me and for my arm they hope. (51:4-5)

For the purposes of our investigation we can dismiss the last *two* three passages, since the third (42:4) is the passage we are trying to clarify, while the fourth (49:1-3) and fifth (51:4-5) are too closely related to the servant texts to provide independent evidence.[13] That leaves the first two. These appear in contexts where the Lord's universal glory is underscored in contradistinction to the vanity of the nations' deities and the powerlessness of their earthly leaders.[14] In the first, God is asserting his status as the one universal God by stating that he did not learn *mišpaṭ* from anyone else, either humans or their supposed deities (40:15-26); in the second, he is ready to appear alongside the nations and their deities (41:21-29) in order to face *mišpaṭ* (here obviously in the sense of judgment) together with them.

These texts lead to the conclusion that *mišpaṭ* in Second-Isaiah bears the connotation of a showdown between the Lord, on the

---

[13] While 51:4-5 is not itself part of a servant poem, its statement that "a *torah* will go forth from me, and my *mišpaṭ* for a light to the nations" closely parallels the first and second ones (see 42:1d, 4c and 49:4b, 6b).

[14] See 40:12-31 and 41:1-7, 21-29.

one hand, and the nations and their deities on the other. This showdown will vindicate him as the sole universal God since it will reveal that Cyrus, the victorious king *of the nations,* was raised up by none other than the Lord himself (41:2-4; 45:1-13; 48:12-15). The same word *mišpaṭ* at once designates both the process (the showdown) and its outcome (God's victory). As for the latter, the "justice" which arises from this "judgment" is more specifically to be understood as the Lord's own *torah*,[15] with which he had originally graced Israel, and under which he is now intending to bring all the nations of the earth, so that both groups may enjoy his everlasting covenant (55:3-5).

If the texts from which we inferred this unique dual meaning of *mišpaṭ* were unrelated to the first servant poem, assigning the same meaning to its use there might be questionable. But such is not the case. A close look at 41:1 and 42:4 will reveal that they form an *inclusio*: in the former, the *'iyyim* are called for a *mišpaṭ,* and in the latter, they await the Lord's *mišpaṭ* expressed in his *torah*.

So the entire passage, 41:1-42:9, is a single literary unit wherein the first servant poem is to be read and understood. Other facts point to this conclusion:

1. The *'iyyim* are addressed directly (second person rather than third person) only twice in Second-Isaiah, in 41:1 and in 49:1. Since 49:1 is the

---

[15] See especially 51:4 where the Lord says: "Listen to me, my people ... for a *torah* will go forth from me, and my *mišpaṭ* for a light to the peoples. My deliverance draws near speedily, my salvation has gone forth ... the coastlands wait for me, and for my arm they hope." Notice the correspondence in terminology with 49:6 where the servant is entrusted with *one* mission to both Israel and the nations, its object being "that my salvation may reach to the end of the earth."

beginning of the second servant poem where the servant himself is speaking, the virtually identical wording of 41:1 may well indicate that the speaker there is not the Lord but the servant, who is calling the *'iyyim* to appear with him for a showdown (*mišpaṭ*). Indeed, during the actual debate with the *'iyyim* God is referred to in the third person (41:21).

2. Following each of the first two poems is a passage that begins with "Thus says the Lord" and addresses the servant in a similar way, which betrays an intended parallelism between them.[16] In the second, the expression "Thus says the Lord" is warranted by the change of speaker from the servant (49:1-6) to God (vv.7-12). In the case of the first poem, however, this change does not make sense unless one assumes that the divine words of 42:1-4 are part of a speech by the servant that started at 41:1 in the same way as the divine words of 49:6 are part of the servant speech in 49:1-6.

3. The word "behold" appears numerous times in 41:1-42:9 (41:11, 15, 24, 29; 42:1). Each of the instances prior to 42:1 introduces a statement by God in support of his claim to be the sole master of both Israel and the nations, so 42:1-4 may well have been intended as yet another such statement.

---

[16] 42:5-9 and 49:7-12, respectively. Compare 42:6 with 49:8, and 42:7 with 49:9a.

The reading of 41:1-42:9 as one literary unit integrates the first servant poem into the entire message of Second-Isaiah. Though endowed with a messianic commission (44:28-45:1), Cyrus is only a cover for God's real messenger, the servant. Cyrus' rise to power and liberation of those subjugated by Babylon, including the Judahites, is just the occasion for the Lord's real message,[17] namely, that he and only he is the master of the world's destiny: the liberator Cyrus as well as the liberated Israel and the liberated nations have only him as their God. The total absence of David as an eschatological figure in Second-Isaiah[18]—as well as in Third-Isaiah, for that matter—is intended to underscore God's direct kingship in the process of the post-exilic restoration. Unlike Ezekiel,[19] in Second-Isaiah it is God *alone* who will be the eschatological ruler, with no intermediary. Chapters 40-55 abound with passages describing the Lord's creative activity or referring to him as king or sole God.[20]

In order to reserve the unique role of eschatological ruler exclusively for himself, God assigns two essentially "kingly" functions to two different individuals, thereby splitting what was thought of as inseparable, and thus leaving neither individual a "king" in the sense of someone like David. The function of leading armies to victory over enemies and the glory and power resulting from that, he gives to Cyrus; the administration of justice (*mišpaṭ*) he allots to the servant.[21] Both of these functions

---

[17] See Jer 1 where the siege of Jerusalem by the Babylonians was only the opportunity for God to show the real siege, that of Jeremiah and his God by Jerusalem.

[18] David is mentioned only once as the historical past figure to whom the promises about to be fulfilled were made (55:3).

[19] See Ezek 34:23-24; 37:24-25 where the new David is God's representative.

[20] 40:12-31; 41:21-29; 42:10-13; 43:8-12, 15-21; 44:6-20, 24-28; 45:9-13; 51:4-11; 52:7-12.

[21] Some key texts which ascribe these functions to the king are: 1 Kg 3:16-28; Ps 45:4-7; 72:1-15; 97:1-12; 99:1-5; 110:5-6.

would be required for any one individual to be considered king in the fullest sense, that is, God's plenipotentiary representative. The two functions, however, are not of equal importance, the former being clearly subservient to the latter. According to 41:1 it is through *mišpaṭ* (in the sense of judgment) that God's victory will be settled, and then it will be through *mišpaṭ* (in the sense of justice) that God will rule and build up the world he has conquered.[22] Hence the superiority of the servant over Cyrus in God's plan: although the Lord will subjugate kings under Cyrus (41:2), "kings[23] shall shut their mouths because of him [the servant]; for that which has not been told them they shall see, and that which they have not heard they shall understand" (52:15). What they will be given to understand is precisely that the servant too will be granted divine victory (53:12a). It is then the servant who, in God's time, will be shown to be his plenipotentiary representative in that he will ultimately combine in himself both divine functions of victory and *mišpaṭ*. Although the actual mission is accomplished through his divine emissary, the glory is due only to God (42:10-17) since, as was already the case with the divine assignee in 9:5-6, it is "the zeal of the Lord of hosts" that "will accomplish this" (v.7).

As such, the basic message of Second-Isaiah is this: the hope of Isaiah will be realized through the intermediacy of a special emissary[24] sent by God in whom he trusted. So why then the expanded and, to the ear, tedious version of the same in order to

---

[22] Notice how the servant's mission is the last in a series of texts introduced with "behold"; the others, which herald Cyrus' rise to power and victory, lead up to it as to a conclusion (see above).

[23] Presumably Cyrus is included.

[24] It is worth pointing out that the verb *naṣar* to speak of God keeping that servant is the same trilateral as the noun *neṣer* (branch; sprout; shoot) that occurs in Is 11:1.

end with another reference to the same servant whose mission is relayed with the same exact words in the original Hebrew, "and I have kept you and given you as a covenant to the people" (42:6; 49:8)? In scripture one often encounters the literary device of underscoring a message by revisiting it twice for a total of three. The hearer is thus forewarned not only twice, but thrice; by the same token the third time is the last chance to heed the message before the eventual verdict of judgment. Consider, for instance, the three stories of harlotry in Ezekiel (chs.16, 20, 23); the three temptations of Jesus (Mt 4:1-11; Lk 4:1-13); the three announcements of the passion of the Son of man (Lk 9:22; 9:43b-45; 18:31-34); the three accounts of Paul's conversion (Acts 9:1-18: 22:5-16; 26:9-18); see especially Paul's statement at the end of 2 Corinthians:

> This is the third time I am coming to you. Any charge must be sustained by the evidence of two or three witnesses. I warned those who sinned before and all the others, and I warn them now while absent, as I did when present on my second visit, that if I come again I will not spare them … Examine yourselves, to see whether you are holding to your faith. Test yourselves. Do you not realize that Jesus Christ is in you?—unless indeed you fail to meet the test! I hope you will find out that we have not failed. But we pray God that you may not do wrong—not that we may appear to have met the test, but that you may do what is right, though we may seem to have failed … I write this while I am away from you, in order that when I come I may not have to be severe in my use of the authority which the Lord has given me for building up and not for tearing down. (13:1-2, 5-7, 10)

Moreover, since the second time round is the penultimate chance for the hearers to understand—especially since the third time precedes or even brings with it the test—it is usually an extensive expansion of what was said the first time in order to give as much opportunity as possible for the hearers to realize the importance of the teaching or the gravity of the matter. A classic example of such is Luke's handling of Jesus' teaching beginning with the first announcement of the passion. The material following that announcement is confined to 21 verses (9:23-43), whereas the teaching following the second announcement extends over nine chapters (9:46 to 18:30) and is filled with many parables special to Luke. In Isaiah, within the expanded version (Is 42:18-49:26) of 40:1-42:17, the author uses the literary device of repetition or even double repetition in order to drill the message into the hearers' minds so there is no chance of misunderstanding, to the tune of, "If I said it once, I've said it a thousand times."

The first reference is to the sin of Israel, the Lord's blind and deaf "servant," which occasioned the destruction of Jerusalem and the punishment into exile (42:18-25). In view of the oracle against Babylon (43:14-21), what follows next is a lengthy passage hailing the Lord as the protector and savior of Israel (43:1-7), which is replete of the vocabulary specific to Second-Isaiah. Two main verbs, *bara'* (heal; make functional; create) and *yaṣar* (form; fashion [from clay as a potter would]), which occur in Genesis 1 and 2, bracket our passage here as *inclusio* since they both are used in 43:1 and 7:

> But now thus says the Lord, he who created (*bore'*) you, O Jacob, he who formed (*yoṣer*) you, O Israel. (v.1)

> every one who is called by my name, whom I created (*bara'ti*) for my glory, whom I formed (*yaṣarti*) and made (*'aśiti* from the root *'aśah*). (v.7)

The verb *'aśah* (make; do) serves to emphasize the function of the first two verbs (*bara'* and *yaṣar*): the Lord is the "producer" of Israel and, by the same token, Israel is his possession: "you are mine (*li-'attah*; mine you are)." (v.1) The combination of these three verbs is intentional. It looks ahead to 45:7 where we hear that the same Lord is actually the "producer" and thus in total control, not only of Israel, but of everything that is and happens: "I form (*yoṣer*) light and create (*bore'*) darkness, I make (*'oseh*) weal and create (*bore'*) woe, I am the Lord, who do (*'oseh*) all these things." That is why, as we shall see, he is the master of Cyrus' destiny (vv.1-6) as well as that of Israel. If Israel is the Lord's, then he is committed to their welfare, as a *go'el* (redeemer) would be, especially when they are in need: "Fear not, for I have redeemed (*ga'alti*) you; I have called you by name, you are mine." (43:1b)

However, such is a double-edged sword. If God "called" Israel "by name," then upon redemption (vv.3-6) each person will have to realize, that he "is called by my name" (v.7a), which means that he would be known as pertaining to God. It is in this sense that one is to understand "witnesses" (*'edim*) in vv.9 and 10 and not in the sense that those saved will "bear witness to" God's salvation whether verbally or through any action on their part. This will be made clear later: "This one will say, 'I am the Lord's,' another will call himself by the name of Jacob, and another will write on his hand, 'The Lord's,' and surname himself by the name of Israel." (44:5)

The real showdown is between the Lord and the other false deities. Those false deities cannot produce witnesses in the nations they rule, who could attest to their power, since such deities never provide salvation to their constituencies (43:9b) the way the Lord does (vv.11, 12b). Moreover, and more importantly, the other deities never proclaim ahead of time their intervention in behalf of their nations (v.9a) as the Lord does (v.12a):

> Let all the nations gather together, and let the peoples assemble. 43
> Who among them can declare this, and show us the former
> things? Let them bring their witnesses to justify them, and let
> them hear and say. It is true. "You are my witnesses," say the Lord,
> "and my servant whom I have chosen, that you may know and
> believe me and understand that I am He. Before me no god was
> formed, nor shall there be any after me. I, I am the Lord, and
> besides me there is no savior. I declared and saved and proclaimed,
> when there was no strange god among you; and you are my
> witnesses, say the Lord. (vv.9-12) 43

And since he is the only functional deity, the Lord is by the same 43
token the deity of all nations and, as such, he can summon Cyrus
against Babylon (v.14). And let Israel beware: "I, I am the Lord,
and besides me there is no savior ... I am the Lord, your Holy
One, the Creator (*bore*) of Israel, your King." (vv.11, 15) The
reason behind this caveat is that Israel was privy to God's
previous intervention at their exodus from Egypt (vv.16-22).
Furthermore, the caveat is necessary since, after the experience of
the exodus, Israel was stubbornly ungrateful (vv.22-28).

As indicated previously,[25] the author uses repetition as a device to
drill his message into the minds of hearers. He does this by
expanding on the features he already covered: compare 44:1-5, 21-
23 with 43:1-7 (the choosing of Israel); 44:6-8 with 43:8-12 (the
Lord is the sole functional deity); 44:9-20 with 41:11-29 (mockery
of the other deities as idols); 44:24-45:8 with 41:1-7 (Cyrus' call by
the one universal God); ch.46 and 47 with 43:14-15 (the fall of

---

[25] See my discussion of 42:18-49:26.

Babylon). However, the author also introduces elements that are central to the book's overall message:

1. At the center of the entire section we have a passage that speaks of the nations' submission to the Lord as universal deity, which is the result of the servant's mission to instruct the nations with God's teaching (42:1, 4, 6; 49:1, 6).

2. What is about to take place is not happenstance, but rather the result of the word communicated long ago (48:1-11).

3. The choice of Cyrus is revisited for the last time (48:12-15) before he disappears completely from the picture to give way to the anonymous messenger who will have center stage thereafter as the sole true servant of the Lord (49:1-7; 52:10-53:12).

4. Just before the announcement of the end of the exile, Israel is reminded that its future safety will lie in abiding by the instruction of its redeemer (48:16-19) which will be communicated through his servant (50:4-11).

It is with this thought in mind that the second lengthy section of Second-Isaiah culminates with the second poem dedicated to that servant (49:1-7).

The Second Servant Poem

49:1 Listen to me, O coastlands, and hearken, you peoples from afar. The Lord called me from the womb, from the body of my mother he named my name. 2 He made my mouth like a sharp sword, in

Revelations! John's vision of Christ

the shadow of his hand he hid me; he made me a polished arrow, in his quiver he hid me away. ³And he said to me, "You are my servant, Israel, in whom I will be glorified." ⁴But I said, "I have labored in vain, I have spent my strength for nothing and vanity; yet surely my right is with the Lord, and my recompense with my God." ⁵And now the Lord says, who formed me from the womb to be his servant, to bring Jacob back to him, and that Israel might be gathered to him, for I am honored in the eyes of the Lord, and my God has become my strength—⁶he says: "It is too light a thing that you should be my servant to raise up the tribes of Jacob and to restore the preserved of Israel; I will give you as a light to the nations, that my salvation may reach to the end of the earth."

As was the case with the first poem, the basic theme of the second poem is the servant's mission to the nations. To begin, the servant addresses his declaration to the *'iyyim* and the "peoples from afar" (v.1a) and, at the end, God explains the ultimate purpose of his servant's mission not only to raise up the tribes of Jacob and restore the preserved of Israel, but also to be "a light to the nations, that my salvation may reach to the end of the earth" (v.6). As an indication of its relative importance, note that this statement quotes God directly, while the mission to Jacob/Israel described in v.5 is not a quotation at all but rather a relative clause identifying the Lord who speaks in v.6.

Still, the mention of the mission to Israel cannot be written off as an insignificant digression, since it does take up one fourth of the poem (vv.5-6a) and begins with the same "called from the womb" formula with which the servant introduced himself in v.1b. Also, v.6 suggests the two missions are closely related, that is, more like two aspects of one mission than two separate

missions.[26] Therefore, understanding the mission to Israel is vital
to understanding the whole poem. As summarized in vv.5b-6a,
the object of that mission is "to bring Jacob back to the Lord ...
that Israel might be gathered to him ... to raise up the tribes of
Jacob and to restore the preserved of Israel." This language is
unlike anything in the first servant poem, but consider the
remarkable similarity between *mišpaṭ*/*torah* and *yešuʿah*/*yešeʿ*
(salvation/victory) as they appear in both of these poems and the
closely related passage 51:4-5: God's *mišpaṭ*/*torah* "goes forth/is
brought forth" (42:1, 3; 51:4) as "a light to the peoples" (51:4),
and the *ʾiyyim* "wait" for it; similarly, his *yešeʿ* "goes forth" (51:5)
because the servant is "a light to the nations" (49:6), and the
ʾiyyim "wait" for it (51:5). The servant who brings God's *mišpaṭ*
/*torah* "to the nations" in the first poem, is instrumental in
making his salvation "reach to the end of the earth" in the
second. Taking into consideration these similarities and the fact
that the word *yešuʿah* also means "victory" (actually its original
meaning),[27] we can conclude that the second poem's setting is
the same as the first's, where the *yešuʿah* (salvation through
victory) is Israel's in the sense that it is wrought by God *for* and
within Israel (41:8-20). Accordingly, the servant's mission is
meant to take place not only for Israel but within it.[28] That this
mission to Israel is itself the content of the servant's mission to
the nations, and not just a preamble to it, can be seen from the
structure of the dialogue between the servant and God:

---

[26] See also 51:4-5, which closely parallels the first two servant poems' phraseology
regarding the mission to the nations, yet is explicitly addressed to Israel.

[27] Compare also the verb *nikbad* (RSV: honored) and the noun *ʿoz* (RSV: strength) at the
end of 49:5. The first means "to be glorified (by God)" and the second has the
connotation of "(divine) power connected with victory."

[28] See my comments earlier on Is 43:9-12.

1. Each of the verses in 49:3-6 displays the same pattern: a statement about the servant's mission (or his call in the case of v.3) is followed by a statement about the positive result or realized purpose of that mission. The mission to Israel is presented in the first part of v.5 and v.6, that is, as part of the "mission statement" in those verses; but the mission to the nations finds expression only in the second part of v.6, that is, in the "result or purpose statement."[29]

2. The mission to Israel in vv.5a and 6a parallels the servant's labor and spending of his strength in v.4a, suggesting that this is actually the part of his mission in which he takes action. But at the same time the notion of effort expended in vain in v.4a also recalls the paradoxical nature of the servant's mission and the idea there that he will carry it out under some kind of pressure or duress, which are characteristics of the mission to the nations in the first poem.

3. The statement concerning the futility of the servant's work in v.4a parallels the term "servant" in v.3a, clearly indicating that the former reflects the essence of what it means to be the Lord's servant.[30] This finds confirmation in the

---

[29] This is clear in the Hebrew original.

[30] If, as seems probable, 49:1-6 is structured according to poetic inversion, this would provide more evidence for the parallel between vv.3 and 4: A/the nations (v.1a); B/the call from the womb (vv.1b-2); C/the person of the servant (v.3); C'/the mission of the servant (v.4); B'/the call from the womb and mission to Israel (v.5); A'/the mission to the nations (v.6).

emphatic "And now" at the beginning of v.5:
now that the servant has fulfilled the conditions
of his mission (v.4), as stipulated by the One who
chose him (v.5), he is made privy to the ultimate
scope of that mission (v.6).[31]

4. In that case, v.6 is not really commissioning the
servant to a new mission. Indeed, how could it be
so if his fate as God's servant was decided long
ago, even from his mother's womb (v.3b, 5a)?
Consequently, even v.3a is to be read not so
much as a commissioning, but rather as a simple
statement of fact, just as it sounds: "You are my
servant." This reading of the text is corroborated
by the servant's reaction, in which he confirms
that statement by recalling what he has done in
the past and expressing his expectation for the
future: "I *have labored* in vain, I *have spent* my
strength for nothing and vanity; *yet surely* my
right is with the Lord, and my recompense with
my God." (v.4) As he pronounces these words,
the servant is positioned, as it were, between
vv.4a and 4b, not at the beginning of v.4. That is
to say, his work as a servant is already behind
him,[32] and he is expressing his confidence[33] that
the Lord who made him what he is, will surely
bring about what he has in mind. It is only after
the servant has performed his allotted task and

---

[31] The "And now" ultimately introduces the statement in v.6 since all of v.5 is a relative clause qualifying the speaker.

[32] Whatever may still lie ahead for him to do—if anything—would only be to carry on what he has already been doing.

[33] Notice the emphatic *'aken* (nevertheless; yet surely).

has reached the point of waiting patiently for God to bring fruition to his apparently fruitless work, that God reveals his ultimate intention (v.6).

"Israel" in Isaiah

The crux that remains to be solved is the designation of the servant as Israel in 49:3: "You are my servant, Israel, in whom I will be glorified." What is perplexing is that same servant is entrusted with a mission *to* Israel in vv.5-6, and especially that he is described with highly individual features such as his being "called from the womb" and "named from his mother's body" (v.1b). So the relevant question pertains to its function in the encompassing argument of Second-Isaiah. The immediate function is to preempt any possibility for the hearer to identify the servant as being Cyrus. Without the "addition" of Israel it would have been quite possible for someone to assume that Cyrus might be the servant of this poem—and by extension the servant of all four poems—since there is specific mention of the raising up of Jacob and the restoration of Israel. Elsewhere, Second-Isaiah unequivocally calls Cyrus the Lord's shepherd (44:28) and anointed (i.e., messiah; 45:1), and consistently presents him as the liberator purposely raised up by God to bring salvation to Israel, the Lord's servant.[34] It is true that Cyrus is not once explicitly termed "servant," while Jacob/Israel is granted that appellative no less than nine times,[35] but the similarities between Cyrus and the protagonist of the four poems would nevertheless have made him a prime candidate for anyone attempting to identify the unnamed servant of the Lord. Cyrus

---

[34] See 41:2-3 in conjunction with vv.8-20; 44:28-45:4; 48:12-15; and 48:20 in conjunction with the second servant poem, which immediately follows it.
[35] 41:8, 9; 42:19; 44:1, 2, 21, 26; 45:4; 48:20.

is, in fact, "beloved" by God (48:14), just as are Israel (43:4) and Abraham (41:8).[36] So the "addition" of Israel in 49:3 makes sense at this juncture especially that Cyrus was just introduced as the medium through whom "the preserved of Israel" (49:6) shall be returned from their exile in Babylon (48:12-22). However, such is a "negative" function. Can one also speak of a "positive" function of the name Israel in 49:3?

In order to answer this question, let me begin by pointing out that, although Jacob and Israel are often used in parallel in Second-Isaiah starting with 40:27, one hears exclusively of Israel after chapter 49 (52:12; 54:5; 55:5). So, at the end of the story of consolation through restoration, God's chosen servant is more particularly known as Israel rather than Jacob. A keen ear will have noticed that already in 44:1-6 "extra value" is given to the name Israel:

[44:1-6] [1]"But now hear, O Jacob my servant, Israel whom I have chosen! [2]Thus says the Lord who made you, who formed you from the womb and will help you: [3]Fear not, O Jacob my servant, Jeshurun whom I have chosen. For I will pour water on the thirsty land, and streams on the dry ground; I will pour my Spirit upon your descendants, and my blessing on your offspring. [4]They shall spring up like grass amid waters, like willows by flowing streams. [5]This one will say, 'I am the Lord's,' another will call himself by the name of Jacob, and another will write on his hand, 'The Lord's,' and surname himself (*yekanneh*)[37] by the name of Israel." [6]Thus says the Lord, the King of Israel and his Redeemer, the Lord of hosts: "I am the first and I am the last; besides me there is no god."

---

[36] Translated as "friend" in RSV.
[37] If read consonantally, the same verb can be parsed as the passive *yekunneh* (be surnamed).

Notice the special importance given to Israel when compared to Jacob. First of all, the "chosen" in v.1 is Israel just as it is in 45:4, and "my people" just as in 43:20. Secondly, as "chosen," the same Israel is "surnamed" *yešurun* (Jeshurun; 44:2) whose meaning is "they will be upright, they will behave uprightly." As such it points ahead to those who will be restored as a "new" Israel when the Lord will "pour his Spirit" upon them (59:21; 63:14; compare with Ezek 37). Thirdly, compared to Jacob, Israel is a special name, a surname (Is 44:5). Aside from Job 32:21 and 22, where it is translated as "flatter, use flattery, and thus deal in a special way," the verb *kinneh* is found only once more in scripture and, no less, in conjunction with Cyrus' mission as God's special messenger "for the sake of my servant Jacob and Israel my chosen": "For the sake of my servant Jacob, and Israel my chosen, I call you by your name, I surname (*'ekanneh*) you, though you do not know me." (45:4)

The dismissal of Jacob in favor of Israel is not so much happenstance as it is programmatic.[38] It begins with the introduction of the "addition" in 49:3 (And he said to me, "You are my servant, Israel, in whom I will be glorified") which forms an *inclusio* with the final mention of Israel in Second-Isaiah: "Behold, you shall call nations that you know not, and nations that knew you not shall run to you, because of the Lord your God, and of the Holy One of Israel, for he has glorified you." (55:5) The intentionality of the *inclusio* is corroborated in that the Lord is also referred to twice as "the Holy One of Israel" in 49:7. Furthermore, the dismissal of Jacob is anti-climactic. After Jacob and Israel are joined in 49:5 and 6, Israel is mentioned on its own in v.7, giving the impression that the cycle ends there:

---

[38] I owe the following to a communication from Mr. Iskandar Abou-Chaar, a colleague in Lebanon.

"Thus says the Lord, the Redeemer of Israel and his Holy One, to one deeply despised, abhorred by the nations, the servant of rulers: 'Kings shall see and arise; princes, and they shall prostrate themselves; because of the Lord, who is faithful, the Holy One of Israel, who has chosen you.'" However, after a long silence concerning both Jacob and Israel, the last verse of chapter 49 refers only to Jacob and with the same tone of victory over the nations, which was heard in v.7 regarding Israel: "I will make your oppressors eat their own flesh, and they shall be drunk with their own blood as with wine. Then all flesh shall know that I am the Lord your Savior, and your Redeemer, the Mighty One of Jacob." (v.26) So the hearers get the impression that Jacob is actually the final denomination [appellative] of the redeemed, an impression that will soon be proven wrong when they realize that Jacob disappears totally from the scene and is supplanted by the thrice mention of Israel in 52:12; 54:5; 55:5. Finally, what is striking about these instances is that, in spite of the stress on God's protecting Israel, nevertheless he is the universal God whose ultimate intention is to include the nations into his new people, a topic that will be the major concern of Third-Isaiah as well as the final scope of the mission of the "servant" (49:6; see also 42, 1, 4, 6).

As for the perceived tension created by the reference of Israel to both the people and the individual servant, it will be resolved in the following chapters 50 and 51.

The Third Servant Poem 50:4 – 10

50:4The Lord God has given me the tongue of those who are taught, that I may know how to sustain with a word him that is weary. Morning by morning he wakens, he wakens my ear to hear as those who are taught. 5The Lord God has opened my ear, and I was not rebellious, I turned not backward. 6I gave my back to the smiters, and my cheeks to those who pulled out the beard; I hid not my face from shame and spitting. ⁷For the Lord God helps me; therefore I have not been confounded; therefore I have set my face like a flint, and I know that I shall not be put to shame; ⁸he who vindicates me is near. Who will contend with me? Let us stand up together. Who is my adversary? Let him come near to me. ⁹Behold, the Lord God helps me; who will declare me guilty? Behold, all of them will wear out like a garment; the moth will eat them up. ¹⁰Who among you fears the Lord and obeys the voice of his servant, who walks in darkness and has no light, yet trusts in the name of the Lord and relies upon his God?

After the second lengthy coverage of the servant's mission, the third time around (50:4-9) the author comes directly to the point. He begins by reminding the hearers that, even in exile, Israel remains God's property (vv.1-3). He never issued them a letter of divorce (v.1) and thus he is still the first in line, the *go'el*, to intervene in their behalf. Their exile is a punishment for their sins, showing them that they are no better than the nations. Such being the case, when he intervenes, his intervention will encompass not only them but also all nations. This will be realized through the sole servant assigned for that mission. In chapters 50-55 Cyrus is not mentioned, nor is Jacob/Israel referred to as "servant." The third servant poem looks like an expansion of 49:4: 50:4-6 correspond to 49:4a (both describe the servant's difficult mission), and 50:7-9 parallel 49:4b (both express the servant's confidence in the Lord). By elaborating on already familiar themes it fills in some of the gaps in the knowledge about the servant.

The servant introduces himself as a *limmud* (disciple; literally, one who is taught) of the Lord. As such, his business is not merely to learn (50:4c) but also to teach others what he himself is taught (v.4ab). In other words, he is assigned (as in 42:4c) the task of propagating the divine instruction or *torah*,[39] a duty typically belonging to king or priest. However, the servant's role is more disciple than teacher: he is taught this *torah*, that is, God's will, *every morning*. In contrast to others who look to a traditional *torah* established in the past and remaining as immutable as the written word used to preserve it, the servant is to *await* God's will in order to be able to dispense it, much as one would await a human king's commands each day. This feature would make of the servant a prophet in the likeness of Amos, Hosea, Isaiah, Jeremiah, and Ezekiel.[40] He even sounds like the ideal prophet, since he does not rebel against anything the Lord tells him and does not turn back from whatever task the Lord assigns to him (50:5).

Verse 6 details the results of the servant's obedience, and by extension the content of the divine commandment to him. If he willingly suffers the indignities described here, it can only be because God's word decreed it. In other words, in the case of the servant, the word of prophecy not only "takes flesh" in the sense that it is fulfilled—as it did with the prophets who preceded him—but also in the more direct sense that it is borne by and expressed in the servant's own person. The third poem thus clarifies the ambiguous, if not cryptic, content of verses 42:4a and 49:4a in the first two poems: it is the very person of the

---

[39] The close connection between the verb *lamad* (to learn) or its cognate *limmed* (to teach) on the one hand, and the *torah* with its commandments, statutes, testimonies, and judgments/ordinances on the other, can be seen from the usual occurrence of the former in conjunction with the latter in Deuteronomy, the book of the *torah* (4:1, 5, 10 [twice], 14; 5:1, 31; 6:1; 11:19, 17:19; 31:12, 13; i.e., 12 out of the 17 instances of *lamad* or *limmed*) and in Ps 119, the hymn to the *torah* and God's word (vv.7, 12, 26, 64, 66, 68, 71, 73, 108, 124, 135, 171; i.e., all instances of *lamad* or *limmed*).

[40] On this difference between the prophetic word and the fixed *torah*, see the Introduction in *OTI₂*.

servant, or, more accurately, this person "put to shame," that expresses God's *torah/mišpaṭ*.[41]

However, God's instructions to the servant must go beyond merely directing him to endure ill use: an integral part of the servant's obedient response is his complete confidence—while being put to shame by others—that God will indeed ultimately vindicate him (50:7).[42] Furthermore, this confidence is rooted in the fact that it is God who willed that he be put to shame, and the Lord will certainly vindicate and declare innocent the one who merely accepted and carried out his will (v.8-9). Thus the content of God's eschatological *torah/mišpaṭ* announced in the first three servant poems is essentially the servant dishonored yet vindicated by God, even in the midst of his dishonor.

But what about the specifics of the servant's experience: do the poems tell us where it takes place or who dishonors him? In fact, they do offer some indications. As we have seen, what the servant experiences is a direct result of his obedience to God's command (vv.5-6). This can hardly be unrelated to the immediately preceding description of his mission as one of teaching (v.4). And where would he teach but among his peers, that is, within Israel? This surmise is supported by the following facts:

1. The preamble to the third poem (50:1-3) is an indictment of Israel for its sins leading up to the

---

[41] Notice the use of *mišpaṭ* in 50:8. The RSV translates *ba'al mišpaṭi* (literally, the master of my judgment; i.e., the one who stands against me during the process of my judgment) into "my adversary."

[42] Notice how the servant's confidence in the Lord's (future) help (v.7a) is expressed as a present reality ("I have not been confounded" and "I have set my face like a flint" in v.7bc) *while* he is being put to shame (vv.5bc-6). Though sometimes translated differently in English versions, the Hebrew verbs in both cases are all in the same past perfect tense, which connotes assuredness.

exile (v.1b) and specifically reminds Israel that the Lord remains its *go'el* (v.2a).[43]

2. The third poem is followed by an appeal to follow the servant's example of confidence in the Lord despite difficulties in v.10, and a word of judgment against those who create those difficulties in v.11, which jibes well with his mission as a teacher/prophet.

3. The following passage 51:1-8 sounds much like the third servant poem (especially 50:4-5) and calls upon Israel to "listen" (51:1, 4a, 7)[44] and "give ear" (v.4a)[45] to the Lord. The similarity of these verses to the servant's commission in 50:4-5 can hardly be happenstance; in this passage God may be asking Israel to hearken to the message he is sending through and in his servant.

4. As discussed above, the third poem points to a mission that is to take place within Israel.

5. Throughout Second-Isaiah, and interspersed among the servant poems, repeated allusions are made to Israel (Jacob) as a servant of the Lord[46] who, time and again, is sinning against him[47] by being blind and deaf to him.[48] God wanted to

---

[43] See above on the notion of *go'el*.

[44] Also translated as "hearken." In vv.1 and 7, it is the same verb *šama'* found also at the end of 49:4.

[45] *he'ezin*, the *hiphil* form of *'azan* from the noun *'ozen* (ear), used at the end of 50:4 and the beginning of 50:5.

[46] 41:8, 9; 42:19; 44:1, 2, 21, 26, 45:4, 48:20.

[47] 42:18-25; 43:22-28; 50:1-3.

[48] 42:18, 19, 20, 23; see also 43:8; 48:8.

make his *torah* known through his servant Israel (42:21), but Israel refused to obey it (v.24). It is the Lord's servant Israel whom the servant of the poems is trying to bring back to the Lord (49:5) and whose tribes he is to raise up and restore (49:6).

Taking the previous points into consideration will help solve the crux we encountered in the reference to the servant as Israel in 49:3. Since the servant's mission is to bring God's justice (*mišpaṭ*) expressed in his law (*torah*) to the nations as well as the remnant of Jacob, he will accomplish this mission inasmuch as he is bred into that teaching and is obedient to it. It is as such that he will gather around him those who will hearken to his words and constitute the new Zion, the new Israel, which will include those who will be obedient from among the nations (66:18-21). In other words, it is inasmuch as he is surrounded by the new Israel that the servant can be considered as the prototype for the members of that new Israel. Just as he has "the tongue of those who are taught (*limmudim*)" by the Lord (50:4), so also "all your [the new Zion's] sons shall be taught (*limmudim*) by the Lord" (54:13).[49] Moreover, ultimately "this is the heritage of the servants of the Lord and their vindication from me, says the Lord" (v.17b). The importance of this statement is that it contains the only instance of "servants" (in the plural) in Second-Isaiah; the followers of the servant's teaching will likewise become servants of the Lord. On the other hand, the heritage that was taken away from the disobedient people (47:6) will be restituted to them through the mission of the servant: "Thus says the Lord: 'In a time of favor I have answered you, in a day of salvation I have helped you; I have kept you and given you as a

---

[49] These are the only two instances of *limmud* in the entire Book of Isaiah.

covenant to the people, to establish the land, to apportion the
desolate heritages.'" (49:8)[50]

The itinerary starting with the "one" and culminating with the
"many" is already evident in the opening of chapter 51:
"Hearken to me, you who pursue deliverance, you who seek the
Lord; look to the rock from which you were hewn, and to the
quarry from which you were digged. Look to Abraham your
father and to Sarah who bore you; for when he was but one I
called him, and I blessed him and made him many." (vv.1-2)
What is definitely striking in this passage is the inclusion of
Sarah with Abraham since it is the sole reference to her in the
Old Testament outside Genesis. It is she, not Abraham, who is
said to "bear" (*teholel*) the children (v.2a). The importance of the
shift from Abraham to Sarah is warranted in that the addressee is
the new Zion (v.3), a city and thus the "mother" of its citizens
and whose husband is either the city god or its king. This view
will be confirmed in 54:1 where Zion is described as "barren"
('*aqarah*)—the only instance of such in the Latter Prophets—just
as Sarah was (Gen 11:30), and has "not been in travail" (*lo' halah*
[from the same verb as *teholel*]; did not bear). On the other
hand, that the universality of the new Zion and new Israel is in
the prophet's purview here is reflected in the reference to Eden
and "the garden of the Lord" (Is 51:3) which harks back beyond
Genesis 11 to Genesis 2:8. Even more, through the mention of
Rahab, the dragon (*tannin*; [the primeval] sea monster), and
"drying up the sea, the waters of the great deep" (51:9-10) the
author is bringing into the picture Genesis 1:1. The functional
differentiation between Zion and Jerusalem[51] is noticeable in

---

[50] These are the sole instances of "heritage" (*nahalah*) in Second-Isaiah.

[51] See earlier, in chapter 2, my discussion of the functional differentiation between Zion
and Jerusalem.

Isaiah 51 in that the former [Zion] appears thrice for underscoring and always in a positive light (vv.3, 11, 16) whereas, in contrast, the latter [Jerusalem] is mentioned only once and as "you who have drunk at the hand of the Lord the cup of his wrath, who have drunk to the dregs the bowl of staggering" (v.17). Finally, just as was the case in 9:7 and 37:32 where we hear that "the zeal of the Lord of hosts will do this," here also it is "the arm of the Lord" (51:5; see also 52:10) that will accomplish what even the faraway coastlands are hoping for, the establishment of God's justice based on his law (51:4-5). It is the awakening of his arm (51:9) that will bring about the awakening of Zion (v.17 and 52:1). He will bring about the consolation (*menaḥem*) he promised to "the son of man, made like grass" (51:12) at the outset of Second-Isaiah: "Comfort (*naḥamu*; console), comfort my people, says your God ... The grass withers, the flower fades, when the breath of the Lord blows upon it; surely the people is grass. The grass withers, the flower fades; but the word of our God will stand for ever." (40:1, 7-8) Worthy of note are the last verses of chapter 51 addressed to the new Zion:

These two things have befallen you—who will condole with ('*anaḥem*; from the same root *niḥem* [console]) you?—devastation and destruction, famine and sword; who will comfort you? Your sons have fainted, they lie at the head of every street like an antelope in a net; they are full of the wrath of the Lord, the rebuke of your God. Therefore hear this, you who are afflicted, who are drunk, but not with wine: Thus says your Lord, the Lord, your God who pleads the cause of his people: "Behold, I have taken from your hand the cup of staggering; the bowl of my wrath you shall drink no more; and I will put it into the hand of your tormentors (*mogayk*; bringing down your back, forcing you to bow),[52] who have said to you, 'Bow down, that we may pass over'; and you have made your back (*gew*) like the ground and like the street for them to pass over." (vv.19-23)

The noun *gew* (back), which is used here to describe an aggressive action with the aim of shaming someone, is the same noun that occurred earlier in the third servant poem: "I gave my back (*gew*) to the smiters, and my cheeks to those who pulled out the beard; I hid not my face from shame and spitting." (50:6) The parallelism is not only striking, but also intended, given that this noun is found only once more in Isaiah with a positive connotation, in Hezekiah's prayer of thanksgiving.[53] The similarity of fate between the servant and the children of the new Zion confirms our earlier findings concerning their becoming ultimately truthful "servants of the Lord" (54:17) and that the naming of the servant as "Israel" (49:3) is made in view of his being a prototype for all the children of Israel.

The second passage heralding the "awakening" of the new Zion (52:1-11) corroborates that salvation will be solely the work of God himself who will return to Zion to comfort (*niham*) her (v.9), as announced at the outset of Second-Isaiah (40:1), and to become her King (52:7),[54] confirming the original vision of Isaiah (6:1). Moreover, as universal King (52:10),[55] he is the absolute master before whom not only kings of the nations "shall

---

[52] From the same root as *gew* (back).

[53] "O Lord, by these things men live, and in all these is the life of my spirit. Oh, restore me to health and make me live! Lo, it was for my welfare that I had great bitterness; but thou hast held back my life from the pit of destruction, for thou hast cast all my sins behind thy back (*gew*)." (38:16-17)

[54] How beautiful upon the mountains are the feet of him who brings good tidings, who publishes peace, who brings good tidings of good, who publishes salvation, who says to Zion, "Your God *reigns* (*malak*, from the root as *melek* [king]."

[55] The Lord has bared his holy arm before the eyes of *all the nations*; and *all the ends of the earth* shall see the salvation [wrought in v.7] of our God.

shut their mouths" (v.15), but also his elect servant shall submit in unconditional obedience—"without opening his mouth," underscored for stress (53:7)—even though "the will (*ḥaphes*; delight, good pleasure) of the Lord was to bruise him and put him to grief" (v.10)![56] Such categorical submission to the will of God as exclusive master of all and everything is precisely the main feature of the fourth and final Servant Poem in Second-Isaiah.

The Fourth Servant Poem 52:13 – 53:12

[52:13]Behold, my servant shall prosper, he shall be exalted and lifted up, and shall be very high. [14]As many were astonished at him—his appearance was so marred, beyond human semblance, and his form beyond that of the sons of men—[15]so shall he startle many nations; kings shall shut their mouths because of him; for that which has not been told them they shall see, and that which they have not heard they shall understand. [53:1]Who has believed what we have heard? And to whom has the arm of the Lord been revealed? [2]For he grew up before him like a young plant, and like a root out of dry ground; he had no form or comeliness that we should look at him, and no beauty that we should desire him. [3]He was despised and rejected by men; a man of sorrows, and acquainted with grief; and as one from whom men hide their faces he was despised, and we esteemed him not. [4]Surely he has borne our griefs and carried our sorrows; yet we esteemed him stricken, smitten by God, and afflicted. [5]But he was wounded for our transgressions, he was bruised for our iniquities; upon him was the chastisement that made us whole, and with his stripes we are healed. [6]All we like sheep have gone astray; we have turned every one to his own way; and the Lord has laid on him the iniquity of

---

[56] This is what Paul fully understood when he stressed that the servant Jesus Christ's obedience to the shameful death on the cross was ultimately that he be exalted "to the glory of God the Father" (Phil 2:5-11).

us all. [7]He was oppressed, and he was afflicted, yet he opened not his mouth; like a lamb that is led to the slaughter, and like a sheep that before its shearers is dumb, so he opened not his mouth. [8]By oppression and judgment he was taken away; and as for his generation, who considered that he was cut off out of the land of the living, stricken for the transgression of my people? [9]And they made his grave with the wicked and with a rich man in his death, although he had done no violence, and there was no deceit in his mouth. [10]Yet it was the will of the Lord to bruise him; he has put him to grief; when he makes himself an offering for sin, he shall see his offspring, he shall prolong his days; the will of the Lord shall prosper in his hand; [11]he shall see the fruit of the travail of his soul and be satisfied; by his knowledge shall the righteous one, my servant, make many to be accounted righteous; and he shall bear their iniquities. [12]Therefore I will divide him a portion with the great, and he shall divide the spoil with the strong; because he poured out his soul to death, and was numbered with the transgressors; yet he bore the sin of many, and made intercession for the transgressors.

This final poem both recapitulates the contents of its predecessors and goes beyond them by offering a new interpretation of the servant's suffering and shame. The new idea can be found at the center of this long passage's chiastic structure:[57]

A/52:13-15: the servant is glorified before kings;
B/53:1-3: the servant suffers and is humiliated;
C/vv.4-6: the servant's suffering is *for the sin of his fellows*;[58]
B'/vv.7-9: the servant's humiliation and suffering are unto death;

---

[57] Chiasm is a literary device resembling an inversion with a center, according to the pattern ABCB'A' or ABCDC'B'A'. The central element has no correspondent and functions as the focal point of the entire structure.

[58] This section's character as a turning point in the poem is announced by the emphatic *'aken* (yet surely) in v.4.

A'/vv.10-12: the servant is glorified before the great and the strong.[59]

Thus, the focus of the fourth servant poem is to be found in section C. Its theme is not even hinted at in the previous poems: the sins of Israel, the disobedient servant of the Lord, are to be expiated by the sufferings of this obedient servant of the Lord. This servant, then, holds the key to the restoration of Israel—which means it will not happen as a result of Israel's own spontaneous repentance and return to God. On the contrary, it appears rather that it will come about despite Israel's persistent disobedience. It is precisely this highly irregular *mišpaṭ* of the Lord that is the stunning news to be carried to the nations, who, in turn, acknowledge it as indeed *mišpaṭ*.

Yet these verses, important as they are, reflect only part of the story. Recognition of the poem's chiastic structure should not obscure the fact that, like any poem, it is meant to be heard from beginning to end. Such progressive hearing will lead to a fuller understanding of the servant's role. The opening verse 52:13 already predicts the servant's eventual triumphal exaltation in no uncertain terms: he will be "exalted" (*yarum*) and "lifted up" (*nissa'*) as high as the divine King himself.[60] Before that, however,

---

[59] A further justification of this chiastic reading can be found in the fact that the servant poem is bracketed by passages dealing with the restored Jerusalem: 51:17-53:12 and ch.54, which would expand the chiasm to ABCDC'B'A' where A and A' would correspond to these sections on the new Jerusalem. In that case, the lengthy passage 51:17-54:17 in which the new Zion is addressed would conclude the "Book of the Consolation of Israel" that was inaugurated with an address to the old Jerusalem about to be redeemed. Besides the reprisal of the topic of consolation (compare 51:19 and 52:9 with 40:1) notice the similarity between 40:9 (Get you up to a high mountain, O Zion, herald of good tidings; lift up your voice with strength, O Jerusalem, herald of good tidings, lift it up, fear not; say to the cities of Judah, "Behold your God!") and 52:7 (How beautiful upon the mountains are the feet of him who brings good tidings, who publishes peace, who brings good tidings of good, who publishes salvation, who says to Zion, "Your God reigns.").

[60] Compare with Is 6:1 where the same verbs *rum* and *nissa'* appear.

he must endure some kind of abasement, which will reduce him to virtually "subhuman" status. Meanwhile, as this story unfolds, the whole course of his fortunes will be widely known, for the radical and apparently inexplicable change in his fortunes will trigger astonishment among the nations.[61] And if the nations are bewildered at this, it is nothing compared to Israel's bewilderment. The servant's peers not only witness the same incomprehensible turn of events (53:1-3), but also are faced with the discovery that his suffering is for their sake; he endures it as a sacrificial lamb for their iniquities (vv.4-6). As for the servant himself, he willingly goes to his death without even opening his mouth (vv.7-9), even though his sentence is apparently the verdict of an oppressive, unjust human *mišpaṭ* (v.8).

After relating the servant's tragic "end," the text then reveals that his sorrows are deliberately orchestrated by God (v.10a). What's more, the success of God's purpose in setting up these events depends wholly on the servant's reaction to it—only if he willingly, unquestioningly accepts God's plan for him, will that plan succeed (v.10b and d).[62] The servant must quietly go to his fate of suffering and death as a sacrificial lamb, an offering for sin (vv.7, 10). Should he lend a deaf ear to God or resist his

---

[61] The phrase "many nations" actually means "all nations" here. The Hebrew *rabbim* (many) often bears the meaning "as many as there are," that is, "all." That it does so in the present context can be gathered from the parallel between "all" in 53:6 and "many" in vv.11 and 12. See also Is 2:2-3 where "all the nations" parallels "many peoples."

[62] Notice the *'im* (if) at the beginning of v.10b: "*if* he makes himself an offering for sin, he shall see his offspring, he shall prolong his days; the will of the Lord shall prosper in his hand." (v.10bcd) The Hebrew *'im* can also be translated "when," as it is in RSV, but the sense is the same: the servant must "make himself" (i.e., it must be his own doing) an offering before the Lord's purpose can prosper. In v.10d the implication of v.10b is made explicit: the "prosperity" (success) of the "will of the Lord" is "in his hand" (in his power; under his control).

command—as his servant Jacob has done so many times—then the divine purpose would not prosper.

The strength of the text's emphasis on the servant's implicit obedience to God's will can be seen in the way the final announcement of his glorification in v.12a is bracketed by v.11b and v.12bc which speak of his voluntary sacrifice. A causal relationship between the voluntary sacrifice and the glorification is asserted through an awkward syntactical construction that makes v.12a the result of both what precedes it and what follows it:

> by his knowledge shall the righteous one, my servant,
> make many to be accounted righteous;
> and he shall bear their iniquities. (v.11b)
> *Therefore* I will divide him a portion with the great,
> and he shall divide the spoil with the strong; (v.12a)
> *because* he poured out his soul to death,
> and was numbered with the transgressors, (v.12b)
> yet he bore the sin of many,
> and made intercession for the transgressors. (v.12c)

The servant's stubbornly consistent silence to suffering gives God free rein to do what he alone can do: vindicate with his *mišpaṭ* the one declared guilty by human *mišpaṭ*, establish glory amid shame and rejection, and grant life where there is death. In contrast to Israel's habitual disobedience "forcing" the Lord's hand,[63] the servant's perfect obedience now gives God the opportunity to do things completely his way, without interference, from beginning to end. In other words, this servant would offer God an absolutely obstruction-free "void" within the realm of the human world and history, wherein God may act as

---

[63] See my comments on Ezek 20 in *C-Ezek* 231-57.

the "Creator" of a new world, his world, the way he wants it: where the impossible is daily bread, and in place of the present reality in which the barren one cannot possibly conceive, "the children of the barren one are more than those of the one that is married" (54:1). Thus, Second-Isaiah conceived the impossible dream: a human clay for God the potter (41:25; 45:9). In the beginning God made humans with earthen clay, but they rebelled and wrecked his world; with Second-Isaiah's human clay, God will be able to implant the new "heavenly" Jerusalem (ch.54) at the heart of the world wreckage.

Sarah, the New Zion

The barren one (54:1; see Gen 11:30) whose habitation is a tent (v.2) is none other than Sarah referred to in chapter 51. The detailed description of the tent with the curtains, cords, and stakes, is clearly intended to bring to mind the only instance of an encounter between God and Sarah in scripture:

> They said to him, "Where is Sarah your wife?" And he said, "She is in the tent." The Lord said, "I will surely return to you in the spring, and Sarah your wife shall have a son." And Sarah was listening at the tent door behind him. Now Abraham and Sarah were old, advanced in age; it had ceased to be with Sarah after the manner of women. So Sarah laughed to herself, saying, "After I have grown old, and my husband is old, shall I have pleasure?" The Lord said to Abraham, "Why did Sarah laugh, and say, 'Shall I indeed bear a child, now that I am old?' Is anything too hard for the Lord? At the appointed time I will return to you, in the spring, and Sarah shall have a son." But Sarah denied, saying, "I did not laugh"; for she was afraid. He said, "No, but you did laugh." (Gen 18:9-15)

The lack of trust on the part of both Sarah and Abraham, who previously laughed at God's promise (17:17), fits perfectly

Jerusalem's attitude (Is 54:6-8; see also 50:1a). Just as in Isaiah the divine deliverance occurs *in spite of* Israel, so also the realization of the divine promise in Genesis takes place *in spite of* Sarah and Abraham who, by the way, are not said to have lain together as was the case between Abraham and Hagar (Gen 16:4). This correct reading of scripture is reflected in Galatians:

> Tell me, you who desire to be under law, do you not hear the law? For it is written that Abraham had two sons, one by a slave and one by a free woman. But the son of the slave was born according to the flesh, the son of the free woman through promise. (4:21-23)

That Paul is sticking closely to the Genesis story is evident in that he does not use here his characteristic opposition between flesh and spirit, which he appeals to a few verses later (v.29). It is as though Sarah conceived Isaac "with the Lord" rather than with Abraham. My readers should not be scandalized at this phraseology since it occurs in scripture itself: "Now Adam knew Eve his wife, and she conceived and bore Cain, saying, 'I have gotten a man with (the help of)[64] the Lord'." (Gen 4:1) If Cain has been conceived "with the Lord" although Adam knew Eve, how much more the phrase applies to the conceiving of Isaac? In turn, such explains Isaiah's use of the metaphor of husband in reference to God (54:5), which metaphor also occurs in Jeremiah where the Lord is said to be the husband of the forefathers (31:32)! Consequently, one can understand both why and how the Isaianic fourth servant poem is recast as the story of the sacrifice of Isaac (Genesis 22:1-19), who carries the wood for his own burnt offering (v.6a) in sheer obedience to his father, and

---

[64] This addition in RSV is not extant in the original and is intended to lessen the impact of the latter on the North American puritan ear. KJV has "I have gotten a man from the Lord."

speaks as well to the action of Abraham's readiness to sacrifice his "only son" (v.2, 12, 16).[65]

Excursus: The Identity of the Servant of the Poems

Thus, the question, "Whom did Second-Isaiah have in mind when speaking of the servant?" is unanswerable if one is expecting in reply the name of a specific person. Rather, the servant is a wishful thought on the prophet's part, an eschatological vision, as it were, which, if or when realized, will "take flesh."[66] The eschatological setting against which the servant is cast makes him the ultimate "end-time" person though whom God will enact his unhindered reign in this world.

Therefore, although Second-Isaiah did not have a specific individual in mind, it remains for the hearer to decide if and in whom his prophecy is fulfilled. So for the hearer of these poems, the servant is someone who lies in the future—and the hearer himself must decide to recognize, acknowledge, and confess someone as that servant. No other way is possible since the servant is essentially silent and thus no answer can be expected from him. If this seems problematic, it cannot be helped; one must remember that the servant is part and parcel of the prophetic word of the poems, which are in turn part and parcel of Second-Isaiah's entire message, and that message is itself characterized as being anything but simple, straightforward, and easy to understand:

> For my thoughts are not your thoughts, neither are your ways my ways, says the Lord. For as the heavens are higher than the earth, so are my ways higher than your ways and my thoughts than your thoughts. For as the rain and the snow come down from heaven,

---

[65] See my comments in C-Gen 151-2.
[66] "If" from a human perspective, "when" from God's perspective.

and return not thither but water the earth, making it bring forth and sprout, giving seed to the sower and bread to the eater, so shall my word that goes forth from my mouth; it shall not return to me empty, but it shall accomplish that which I purpose, and prosper in the thing for which I sent it. (55:8-11)[67]

Nevertheless, the hearer is called upon to obey God's word, even if he does not comprehend it totally. This message is embedded within an appeal to the (willfully deaf) servant, Israel, to "hearken," "incline the ear," and "hear," so that "your soul may live" (55:2-3).[68] The result of such obedient listening would be Israel's "glorification" by the Lord and its transformation into a refuge for "the nations" (v.5).[69] One can only conclude that Second-Isaiah already presupposes his future hearers' difficulties in identifying the servant: the "advent" of the Lord's servant will have as its corollary a challenge to Israel to "incline the ear" and acknowledge that the Lord's design did prosper at the servant's hand; only then will God's *mišpaṭ* be realized in the eyes of the nations, who will then flock to the new Zion.

In the story of Israel after the time of Second-Isaiah, this did happen once—and only once—when a number of Jews in 1st century A.D., under the leadership of Paul, confessed that God's design was realized in Jesus of Nazareth,[70] who was put to a

---

[67] Notice the same idea of God's purpose or will "prospering," which we find in 53:10d in reference to the servant. The Hebrew behind "purpose" here and "will" in 53:10d is the same verb *ḥapheṣ*. Likewise, the words for "prosper" here and in 53:10d are just different forms of the same verb (perfect *hiṣliaḥ*, imperfect *yiṣlaḥ*).

[68] Contrast with 53:12 where the servant's obedience leads him to "pour out his soul to death" for the sake of his peers' iniquities and sins (vv.11-12).

[69] Compare with the second poem (49:1-6) where the Lord will be "glorified" in his servant, the "light to the nations."

[70] Actually, the choice of Nazareth as the city of Jesus has to do with its reflecting in Greek the three consonants *nṣr* of the Hebrew *neṣer* (branch), the metaphoric reference

shameful death and afterward was vindicated in glory. The leaders of that community of Jewish "believers" in Jesus, as the Lord's eschatological servant, adopted in their writings the same verb "evangelize" (*bisser-evangelizomai*) with which Second-Isaiah characterized his entire message as "good news."[71] Thus, Second-Isaiah's prophetic word requiring trust in the Lord's final *mišpaṭ* finds its realization in another word, the apostolic word, which uses the prophetic vocabulary and also requires trust that the Lord did implement his final *mišpaṭ*. The Apostle Paul characterizes this process as a movement *ek pisteōs eis pistin* (from [one stand of] trust to [another stand of] trust; Rom 1:17). The trust he has in mind in Romans is in the one and same God whose "*gospel* he promised beforehand through his prophets in the holy scriptures,[72] concerning his Son ... designated as Son of God in power according to the Spirit of holiness by his resurrection from the dead" (1:1-4). It is this "gospel" that is "the power of God for salvation to every one who has faith (*pistevonti*; has trust), to the Jew first and also to the Greek.[73] For in it the righteousness [i.e., *mišpaṭ*] of God is revealed *ek pisteōs eis pistin*." (1:16-17) The Jew is first, since he is already bound by the prophetic scripture requiring trust in the *promised* divine word; the Gentile begins by acknowledging the prophetic scripture as the *divine word* entailing a promise. However, Jew

---

to the messiah in Is 11:1: "There shall come forth a shoot from the stump of Jesse, and a branch (*neṣer*) shall grow out of his roots."

[71] It brackets the entire "Book of Consolation" (see 40:9; 52:7).

[72] The intimate connection between the word of promise and the gospel as word of fulfillment of that promise, is evidenced by the prominence of Second-Isaiah in Paul's mind when he speaks of the "mechanism" of the apostolic proclamation and its reception further in the same epistle (Rom 10:17). Compare that text especially with 52:7 and 53:1, that is, the fourth servant poem and its immediate context.

[73] Recall the comments above on 55:2-5, where Israel is called to "hear" in order that it may itself "live" and then become a refuge for "the nations."

and Gentile are on a par; both are required to *trust* that the
promised divine word was *fulfilled* in Jesus the Christ, *as preached
by Paul.* Worthy of note in this regard is that in linking Isaiah 54
to the Genesis story of Sarah's begetting of Isaac, Paul concludes
with "Now we, brethren, like Isaac, are children of promise"
(Gal 4:28), which in turn introduces his reference to the
persecution of Isaac as "born according to the Spirit" in order to
speak of his contemporary situation. That is why, ultimately "as
the rain and the snow come down from heaven, and return not
thither but water the earth, making it bring forth and sprout,
giving seed to the sower and bread to the eater, so shall my word
be that goes forth from my mouth; it shall not return to me
empty, but it shall accomplish that which I purpose, and prosper
in the thing for which I sent it" (Is 55:10-11).

Part III

Isaiah Chapters 56-66

Chapter 9

Post-Exilic Zion

If the first part of Isaiah reflects a pre-exilic setting and the second part an exilic background, the third part (chs.56-66) fits a post-exilic context when the leadership of the people falls into the hands of the priests in the absence of kings (61:6; 66:6, 21).[1] In the second part we repeatedly heard of the special mission of the Lord's emissary to the exiles reminding them that they were punished because they had neglected the Law. The realm of this emissary's mission also encompassed all nations, including those far away isles, inviting them also to submit to the Law in order to share in the inheritance of the new Zion together with the remnant of Israel. As evidenced in the Books of Jonah and Ezra (chs.9-10), for many Jews, the thought of integration of non-Jews into final divine salvation was hard to swallow during the post-exilic period. This explains why the third part of Isaiah specifically revolves around the full inclusion of the "foreigners" and brackets Isaiah 56-66 as an *inclusio*:

> Let not the foreigner who has joined himself to the Lord say, "The Lord will surely separate me from his people"; and let not the eunuch say, "Behold, I am a dry tree." For thus says the Lord: "To the eunuchs who keep my sabbaths, who choose the things that please me and hold fast my covenant, I will give in my house and within my walls a monument and a name better than sons and daughters; I will give them an everlasting name which shall not be cut off. And the foreigners who join themselves to the Lord, to minister to him, to love the name of the Lord, and to be his

---

[1] Compare with Ezekiel 40-48, Zechariah, Haggai and Malachi.

servants, every one who keeps the sabbath, and does not profane
it, and holds fast my covenant." (Is 56:3-6)

For I know their works and their thoughts, and I am coming to
gather all nations and tongues; and they shall come and shall see
my glory, and I will set a sign among them. And from them I will
send survivors to the nations, to Tarshish, Put, and Lud, who
draw the bow, to Tubal and Javan, to the coastlands afar off, that
have not heard my fame or seen my glory; and they shall declare
my glory among the nations. And they shall bring all your
brethren from all the nations as an offering to the Lord, upon
horses, and in chariots, and in litters, and upon mules, and upon
dromedaries, to my holy mountain Jerusalem, says the Lord, just
as the Israelites bring their cereal offering in a clean vessel to the
house of the Lord. And some of them also I will take for priests
and for Levites, says the Lord. (66:18-21)

However, this inclusion of foreigners is contingent on their
abiding by God's *ṣedaqah* (righteousness) and *mišpaṭ* (just
judgment; justice), as is clear from the opening verse: "Thus says
the Lord: 'Keep justice (*mišpaṭ*), and do righteousness
(*ṣedaqah*), for soon my salvation will come, and my deliverance
(*ṣedaqah*) be revealed." (56:1) Since both *mišpaṭ* and *ṣedaqah* are
legal terms and thus pertain to the divine law, it stands to reason
that the immediately following verse intended that *all human
beings* adhere to "keeping the sabbath," which is the day when
the Law is read aloud to the congregated people. This is
corroborated by the occurrences of "sabbath" in Isaiah. Except
for its mention in the introductory chapter (1:13) all other
instances of sabbath are found exclusively in Third-Isaiah (56:2,
4, 6; 58:13; 66:23) and bracket those chapters just as
"foreigners" and "nations" do:

Blessed is the man who does this, and the son of man who holds it fast, who keeps the sabbath, not profaning it, and keeps his hand from doing any evil.[2] (56:2)

From new moon to new moon, and from sabbath to Sabbath, all flesh shall come to worship before me, says the Lord. (66:23)

Consequently, the function of the third part of the book is to ensure that what applied to Jacob still applies to the "remnant" of Jacob and *to the nations as well.* That is why the special messenger of Second-Isaiah (chs.42, 49, 50, and 53) reappears at the center of Third-Isaiah (61-1-6). At the end of the book, we shall hear that aliens and foreigners will join the children of Israel in the priestly service of the new Zion (66:21).

That Third-Isaiah pertains to the post-exilic period finds further corroboration in chapter 58 that has a special lengthy passage dealing with false fasting, followed by two verses dealing with the disregard of the sabbath:

Cry aloud, spare not, lift up your voice like a trumpet; declare to my people their transgression, to the house of Jacob their sins … Behold, in the day of your fast you seek your own pleasure, and oppress your workers. Behold, you fast only to quarrel and to fight and to hit with wicked fists. Fasting like yours this day will not make your voice to be heard on high. Is such the fast that I choose, a day for a man to humble himself? Is it to bow down his head like a rush, and to spread sackcloth and ashes under him? Will you call this a fast, and a day acceptable to the Lord? Is not this the fast that I choose: to loose the bonds of wickedness, to undo the thongs of the yoke, to let the oppressed go free, and to break every yoke? Is it not to share your bread with the hungry, and bring the homeless poor into your house; when you see the

---

[2] See my detailed discussion in *C-Ezek* 245-54 concerning the sabbath and its profanation in Ezek 20.

naked, to cover him, and not to hide yourself from your own
flesh? (vv.1, 4-7)

If you turn back your foot from the sabbath, from doing your
pleasure on my holy day, and call the sabbath a delight and the
holy day of the Lord honorable; if you honor it, not going your
own ways, or seeking your own pleasure, or talking idly; then you
shall take delight in the Lord, and I will make you ride upon the
heights or the earth; I will feed you with the heritage of Jacob your
father, for the mouth of the Lord has spoken. (vv.13-14).

There is no earlier reference to fasting in the book. Just like the
sabbath, fasting is debated in several post-exilic prophetic
passages (Joel 1:14; 2:12-17; Zech 7:1-6; 8:18-19). However,
what makes the issue of fasting even more pertinent for our
discussion, rather than that of the sabbath, is that there is no
mention at all of fasting in the Law. Thus, fasting is not a legal
prescription; it is solely an outward expression of inward
repentance.[3] Jeremiah 14:11-12 and 36:5-10 are only apparent
exceptions to this since they deal with the period when the exile
was imminent, and God's decision was already made and
proclaimed. However, in the first case (14:11-12), fasting is
irrelevant and, in the second (36:5-10), it is shown to be bogus
since, upon hearing the scroll containing "all the words of the
Lord which he had spoken to him [Jeremiah]," the king shreds
and burns it (v.23), although the reading took place on a day of
fasting (vv.6 and 9).

All the preceding points in one direction: by following the
statutes of God's will inscribed in his law and read on the
sabbath, the nations as well as Israel are to truly repent of their

---

[3] See, e.g., 1 Sam 7:6; 31:11-13; 2 Sam 1:11-12; 12:15-23.

evil deeds and vow to circumcise their hearts rather than their foreskins as the Lord required in Deuteronomy:

> And now, Israel, what does the Lord your God require of you, but to fear the Lord your God, to walk in all his ways, to love him, to serve the Lord your God with all your heart and with all your soul, and to keep the commandments and statutes of the Lord, which I command you this day for your good? ... Circumcise therefore the foreskin of your heart, and be no longer stubborn. (Deut 10:12-13, 16)

> If your outcasts are in the uttermost parts of heaven, from there the Lord your God will gather you, and from there he will fetch you; and the Lord your God will bring you into the land (earth) which your fathers possessed (inherited), that you may possess (inherit) it; and he will make you more prosperous and numerous than your fathers. And the Lord your God will circumcise your heart and the heart of your offspring, so that you will love the Lord your God with all your heart and with all your soul, that you may live. (30:4-6)

This is why in the new Zion the "uncircumcised" will not be welcome: "Awake, awake, put on your strength, O Zion; put on your beautiful garments, O Jerusalem, the holy city; for there shall no more come into you the uncircumcised and the unclean." (Is 52:1) If such applied to the remnant of Israel in Second-Isaiah, all the more it applies to the nations in the third part of the book where they will join themselves to the Lord in his one house of prayer on his holy mountain as already promised in 2:2-4.

Yet post-exilic Jerusalem is no better than the pre-exilic one, and is depicted in the same terms. The corrupt leadership (56:10-57:2) leads the people away from true worship into idolatry:

His watchmen are blind, they are all without knowledge; they are
all dumb dogs, they cannot bark, dreaming, lying down, loving to
slumber. The dogs have a mighty appetite; they never have
enough. The shepherds also have no understanding; they have all
turned to their own way, each to his own gain, one and all ... The
righteous man perishes, and no one lays it to heart; devout men
are taken away, while no one understands ... Whom did you
dread and fear, so that you lied, and did not remember me, did
not give me a thought? Have I not held my peace, even for a long
time, and so you do not fear me? ... When you cry out let, your
collection of idols deliver you! (56:10-11; 57:1, 11, 13a)

There is hope "for he who takes refuge in me shall possess the
land (receive the land as inheritance; *yinḥal*), and shall inherit
(*yiraš*) my holy mountains" (v.13b).[4] Those who take refuge in
the Lord, "the high (*ram*) and lofty (*niśśa'*) One, whose name is
Holy (*qadoš*)" (v.15a; compare with 6:1, 3) are solely those who
have a reason to do so: "I dwell in the high and holy place, and
also with him who is of a contrite and humble spirit, to revive
the spirit of the humble, and to revive the heart of the contrite."
(57:15b) The centrality of this thought is confirmed by its
reappearance at the end of the book where again the temple
leadership is criticized (66:1-4): "But this is the man to whom I
will look, he that is humble and contrite in spirit, and trembles
at my word." (v.2b) Furthermore, the inheritance will be
inclusive of those "far or near" and will entail the peace of God
in his city (v.19). However, the "wicked" (*reša'im*) will not enjoy
that peace (vv.20-21).

---

[4] The two verbs *naḥal* and *yaraš* are the two main verbs used in Joshua to speak of the
gift of the earth of Canaan granted by God to whom he wills. See my comments in *C-
Josh* 44-51.

In chapter 58 the wicked are specifically introduced as those who do not hold true fasting (vv.1-12), that is, do not truly repent by following the statutes of the Law read to them on the sabbath (vv.13-14): "Behold, you fast only to quarrel and to fight and to hit with wicked (*reša'*) fist. Fasting like yours this day will not make your voice to be heard on high ... Is not this the fast that I choose: to loose the bonds of wickedness (*reša'*), to undo the thongs of the yoke, to let the oppressed go free, and to break every yoke?" (vv.4, 6)[5] Humble and contrite is he who repents; the wicked are the non-repentant. This can be heard in the lengthy "psalm of repentance" in chapter 59:

> Behold, the Lord's hand is not shortened, that it cannot save, or his ear dull, that it cannot hear. But your iniquities have made a separation between you and your God, and your sins have hid his face from you so that he does not hear. For your hands are defiled with blood and your fingers with iniquity; your lips have spoken lies, your tongue mutters wickedness. No one enters suit justly, no one goes to law honestly; they rely on empty pleas, they speak lies, they conceive mischief and bring forth iniquity ... The way of peace they know not, and there is no justice in their paths; they have made their roads crooked, no one who goes in them knows peace. Therefore justice is far from us and righteousness does not overtake us; we look for light, and behold, darkness, for brightness, but we walk in gloom ... For our transgressions are multiplied before thee, and our sins testify against us; for our transgressions are with us, and we know our iniquities; transgressing, and denying the Lord, and turning away from following our God, speaking oppression and revolt, conceiving and uttering from the heart lying words. (vv.1-4, 8-9, 12-13)

---

[5] These are the only instances of the root *rš'* in Third- Isaiah.

Repentance from the old ways is required in the "new" everlasting covenant, which God will establish at the end. Compare the wording of 59:21 with that of the "new" covenant that is promised in Ezekiel:

a new heart

> And as for me, this is my covenant with them, say the Lord: my spirit which is upon you, and my word which I have put in your mouth, shall not depart out of your mouth, or out of the mouth of your children, or out of the mouth of your children's children, says the Lord, from this time forth and for evermore. (Is 59:21)

> And I will give them one heart, and put a new spirit within them; I will take the stony heart out of their flesh and give them a heart of flesh, that they may walk in my statutes and keep my ordinances and obey them; and they shall be my people, and I will be their God. (Ezek 11:19-20)

> A new heart I will give you, and a new spirit I will put within you; and I will take out of your flesh the heart of stone and give you a heart of flesh. And I will put my spirit within you, and cause you to walk in my statutes and be careful to observe my ordinances. (Ezek 36:26-27)

Isaiah 60

It is precisely at this juncture that the new Zion is summoned to "arise" and "shine (in splendor)" in the light bestowed upon her by the glory of her God (60:1, 19). From the sinful "city of David" she is to be transformed into the "City of the Lord, the Zion of the Holy One of Israel" (v.14), a city where divine peace is ensured through righteousness (v.17b), which requires the ceasing of violence against the poor (v.18a; see earlier 59:6d), and where the salvation wrought by God will produce the rightful praise due him (60:18b). Moreover, those who shall inherit the earth[6] are exclusively the righteous ones who alone are God's people in the image of the chosen one, the "shoot" (*neṣer;* 11:1) who will lead them: "Your people shall all be righteous; they shall inherit the earth for ever, the shoot (*neṣer*) of my planting, the work of my hands." (60:21)

Flanked by the two chapters (60 and 62) concerning the new Zion is the passage about the messenger who will declare and bring about this new reality:

Isaiah 61:1-7

The Spirit of the Lord God is upon me, because the Lord has anointed me to bring good tidings to the afflicted; he has sent me to bind up the brokenhearted, to proclaim liberty to the captives, and the opening of the prison to those who are bound; to proclaim the year of the Lord's favor, and the day of vengeance of our God; to comfort all who mourn; to grant to those who mourn in Zion—to give them a garland instead of ashes, the oil of gladness instead of mourning, the mantle of praise instead of a faint spirit; that they may be called oaks of righteousness, the planting of the Lord, that he may be glorified. They shall build up the ancient ruins, they shall raise up the former devastations; they shall repair the ruined cities, the devastations of many generations. Aliens shall stand and feed your flocks, foreigners shall be your plowmen and vinedressers; but you shall be called the priests of the Lord, men shall speak of you as the ministers of our God; you shall eat the wealth of the nations, and in their riches you shall glory. Instead of your shame you shall have a double portion, instead of dishonor you shall rejoice in your lot;

---

[6] RSV has "shall possess the land." Its 20th century "zionist" bias is evident in that not only does it translate *naḥal* into "possess" (57:13b) but it also translates here *yaraš* into "possess" in spite of the fact that it rendered it earlier as "inherit" (57:13b). See for detail on this matter my comments in *C-Josh* 44-51.

therefore in your land you shall inherit (*yirašu*)[7] a double portion; yours shall be everlasting joy. (61:1-7)

This new reality was already announced at the beginning of Second-Isaiah:

Comfort (*naḥamu*), comfort (*naḥamu*) my people, says your God ... Get you up to a high mountain, O Zion, herald of good tidings (*mebaśśeret*); lift up your voice with strength, O Jerusalem, herald of good tidings (*mebaśśeret*), lift it up, fear not; say to the cities of Judah, "Behold your God!" (40:1, 9)

The parallelism between these chapters 61 and 40 is further evident in that the "double" portion in the heritage (61:7) corresponds to the "double" punishment (40:1). The doubling of the recompense can be actually "heard" in the double description of the new Zion in chapters 60 and 62 that bracket chapter 61.

The discernment between the righteous and the wicked is the result of God's final judgment of all people (63:1-6), which reflects his universal hegemony even over all the other deities (Ps 82). His depiction as coming from Edom (*'edom*; Is 63:1) has to do with the fact that the Hebrew trilateral *'dm* refers to the color red (*'adom*; v.2), which is the color of the shed blood that is compared to the red grapes pressed into wine (vv.3, 6).[8] In view of the radicalism of the divine judgment, the hearers are invited to repentance (64:3-11) in recognition of God's goodness toward them that allowed them a second chance (63:7-64:2). And such goodness lies in his being their "father" even beyond Abraham and Jacob: "For thou art our Father, though Abraham does not

---

[7] RSV has "possess."

[8] This is a classic metaphor (Is 25:6; 49:26; Jer 13:12-14; 25:15-16; Lam 1:15; Joel 3:13; Zech 9:15).

know us and Israel does not acknowledge us; thou, O Lord, art our Father, our Redeemer from of old is thy name." (63:16) After all it was the disobedience of Jacob that caused their predicament. However, the hearers are to beware. True fatherhood does not preclude but essentially entails the authority of judgment and instructional punishment (64:7-8). God remains the potter and they the clay in his hands (v.8; see earlier 29:16; 41:25; 45:9): "I form light and create darkness, I make weal and create woe, I am the Lord, who do all these things." (45:7) In the following chapters (65 and 66), one again hears a lengthy passage (66:1-17) of the upcoming universal judgment that will include post-exilic Jerusalem. This scriptural staple leaves its stamp at the end of the book where, after the depiction of the new Zion (vv.18-21) and even "the new heavens and the new earth which I [the Lord] will make" (vv.22-23), the hearers are struck with an ominous verse: "And they shall go forth and look on the dead bodies of the men that have rebelled against me; for their worm shall not die, their fire shall not be quenched, and they shall be an abhorrence to all flesh." (v.24) This is a reminder not to imagine that one can close the scroll and set it aside, so to speak. It is, in fact, a call to go back to the opening statement of judgment at the beginning of the book (1:2-3) and listen again to the entire Isaianic message. Put otherwise, the Book of Isaiah was intentionally conceived as a recurring and never-ending caveat for all nations as well as for the children of Jacob. It is indeed a masterpiece.

Further Reading

Commentaries and Studies

Baltzer, K. *Deutero-Isaiah.* Hermeneia. Minneapolis: Fortress, 2001.

Beyer, B. *Encountering the Book of Isaiah: A Historical and Theological Survey.* Encountering Biblical Studies. Grand Rapids: Baker Academic, 2007.

Blenkinsopp, J. *Isaiah 1-39: A New Translation with Introduction and Commentary.* Anchor Bible. New York: Doubleday, 2000.

Childs, B. S. *Isaiah.* OTL. Louisville: Westminster John Knox, 2001.

Goldingay, J. *Isaiah.* NIBCOT Peabody, MA: Hendrickson, 2001.

Goldingay, J. and Payne, D. *Isaiah 40-55: A Critical and Exegetical Commentary,* 2 vols. ICC. London/New York: T & T Clark, 2006.

Goulder, M. D. *Isaiah as Liturgy.* Burlington, VT: Ashgate, 2004.

Firth, D. and Williamson, H. G. M., eds. *Interpreting Isaiah: Issues and Approaches.* Downers Grove, IL: InterVarsity Press, 2009.

Leclerc, T. L. *Yahweh is Exalted in Justice: Solidarity and Conflict in Isaiah.* Minneapolis: Fortress, 2001.

Lessing, R. R. *Isaiah 4-55.* Concordia Commentary. St Louis: Concordia, 2011.

Moyse, S. and Menken M. J. J., eds. *Isaiah in the New Testament.* London/New York: Continuum, 2005.

Oswalt, J. N. *Isaiah.* NIV Application Commentary. Grand Rapids, MI: Zondervan, 2003.

Quinn-Miscall, P. D. *Reading Isaiah: Poetry and Vision.* Louisville/London/Leiden: Westminster John Knox, 2001.

Articles

Assis, E. "Why Edom? On the Hostility Towards Jacob's Brother in Prophetic Sources." *Vetus Testamentum* 56 (2006) 1-20.

Baloyi, M. E. "The Unity of the Book of Isaiah: Neglected Evidence (Re-) considered." *Old Testament Essays* 20 (2007) 105-27.

Baltzer, K. "The Book of Isaiah." *Harvard Theological Review* 103 (2010) 261-70.

Barré, M. L. "A Rhetorical-Critical Study of Isaiah 2:12-17." *Catholic Biblical Quarterly* 65 (2003) 522-34.

Berges, U. "The Literary Construction of the Servant in Isaiah 40-55: A Discussion about Individual and Collective Identities." *Scandinavian Journal of the Old Testament* 24 (2010) 28-38.

Blenkinsopp, J. "Judah's Covenant with death (Isaiah xxvii 14-22)." *Vetus Testamentum* 50 (2000) 272-83.

Blenkinsopp, J. "The Cosmological and Protological Language of Deutero-Isaiah." *Catholic Biblical Quarterly* 73 (2011) 493-510.

Flynn, S. W. "Where is YHWH in Isaiah 57,14-15." *Biblica* 87 (2006) 358-70.

Flynn, S. W. "'A House of Prayer for All Peoples': The Unique Place of the Foreigner in the Temple Theology of Trito-Isaiah." *Theoforum* 37 (2006) 5-24.

Fried, L. S. "Cyrus the Messiah." *Bible Review* 19 (5, 2003) 24-31, 44.

Gardner, A.E "The Nature of the New Heavens and New Earth in Isaiah 66:22." *Australian Biblical Review* 50 (2002) 10-67.

Goulder, M. "'Behold my servant Jehoiachin'." *Vetus Testamentum* 52 (2002) 175-90.

Hutton, J, M. "Isaiah 51:9-11 and the Rhetorical Appropriation and Subversion of Hostile Theologies." *Journal of Biblical Literature* 126 (2007) 271-303.

Isbel, C. D. "The Limmûdîm in the Book of Isaiah." *Journal for the Study of the Old Testament* 34 (2009) 99-109.

Jacobson, R. A. "Unwelcome words from the Lord: Isaiah's Messages." *Word and World* 19 (1999) 125-32.

Kratz, R. G. "Israel in the Book of Isaiah." *Journal for the Study of the Old Testament* 31 (2006) 103-28.

Landy, F. "Torah and Anti-Torah: Isiah 2:2-4 and 1:10-26." *Biblical Interpretation* 11 (2003) 317-34.

Leuchter, M. "Tyre's '70 Years' in Isaiah 23,15-18." *Biblica* 87 (2006) 412-17.

Macchi, J.-D. "'Ne reassesses plus les choses d'autrefois'. Esaïe 43,16-21, un surprenant regard deutero-ésaïen sur le passé." *Zeitschrift für die Alttestamentliche Wissenschaft* 121 (2009) 225-41.

McInnes, J. "A Methodological Reflection on Unified Readings of Isaiah." *Colloquium* 42 (2010) 67-84.

Nielsen, K. "'From Oracles to Canon—and the Role of Metaphor." *Scandinavian Journal of the Old Testament* 17 (2003) 22-33.

Niskanen, P. "Yhwh as Father, Redeemer, and Potter in Isaiah 63:7-64:11." *Catholic Biblical Quarterly* 68 (2006) 397-407.

O'Kane, M. "Concealment and Disclosure in Isaiah 28-33." *Revue Biblique* 113 (2006) 481-505.

Oswalt, J. N. "Isaiah 60-62: The Glory of the Lord." *Calvin Theological Journal* 40 (2005) 95-103.

Oswalt, J. N. "The Nations in Isaiah: Friend or Foe; Servant or Partner." *Bulletin for Biblical Research* 16 (2006) 41-51.

Smillie, G. R. "Isaiah 42:1-4 in Its Rhetorical Context." *Bibliotheca Sacra* 162 (2005) 50-65.

Sylva, D. "The Isaian Oracles against the Nations." *The Bible Today* 44 (2006) 215-19.

Terblanche, M. D. "Abraham (Does not) Know(s) Us: An Intertextual Dialogue in the Book of Isaiah." *Old Testament Essays* 24 (2011) 255-83.

Walton, J. "The Imagery of the Substitute King Ritual in Isaiah's Fourth Servant Song." *Journal of Biblical Literature* 122 (2003) 734-43.

Wodecki B. "Jerusalem—Zion in the Texts of Proto-Isaiah." *Polish Journal of Biblical Research* 1 (2000) 89-106.